EXIT STAGE 4

Allyson Rothburd

Cover design by: Art Painter
Library of Congress Control Number: 2018675309
Printed in the United States of America

All procedes of the sale of this book will be donated to the American Cancer Society or Juvenile Diabetes Research Foundation

CONTENTS

Exit Stage 4

Allyson Rothburd

PREFACE

This is not a work of fiction. Allyson wrote this beginning about 2001-2003 after she was told of a diagnosis of Stage 4 breast cancer. I had completely forgotten about this manuscript until I stumbled upon it while going through a closet in the last days of Allyson's life. Allyson was always writing. Poems, kid's stories, short paragraphs. Literary puttering if you will. She did get a children's book published in 1999, "Grandparents are Special," in memory of and honoring her maternal grandparents, especially her grandmother.

I don't remember my thoughts on this memoir when she first showed it to me, but if my reaction was anything like it was reading it now, I'm sure I encouraged her to get it published. She didn't do that. She felt that some of the events were personal and she was reluctant to share them. I think she wrote this to expunge some of her demons.

On rereading this memoir, I am incredulous of some of the situations Allyson and her sister experienced and endured. It has never ceased to amaze me that Allyson grew up to be a warm, loving, caring, kind hearted, person without any bitterness despite her early life.

The events depicted in this manuscript are real. The people mentioned are real; their names have not been changed.

I had heard these stories told many times during our marriage, and believe every word that she has written. Whether the dialogue is true to the events cannot be determined, but I presumed it accurate represents what actually transpired.

PROLOGUE

Vacations are wonderful! Even though you leave the telephone number of where you will be staying with those you have left at home, you know there is a ninety-nine percent chance that no one will call you. The scenery is always different, no matter where you are. If you feel like talking to the strangers on the street or in the shops, you can do so. If you don't want to, you can walk for miles in silence.

During Presidents' week 2001, my husband and I and our friends, Judy and Larry Engelberg, and their two daughters flew from New York to Lake Tahoe for a week of skiing and relaxation. My husband and I took one condominium; the Engelberg's took another. I missed our own daughter not coming with us, but colleges never seem to have vacations that coincide with the rest of the world. Besides, she would be out skiing in Colorado in another month, so I didn't feel that badly.

Before I go on, just let me set the record straight to avoid any confusion that you might have. I said we flew to Lake Tahoe for a week of skiing and relaxation. It is my husband and the Engelberg's who ski – I'm here to relax, though many of you would argue with me and tell me that skiing is relaxing – I never caught on to that concept. To walk to the slopes carrying your heavy, cumbersome equipment I feel negates the pleasure one gets while standing at the top of the mountain while inhaling the crisp air and maintaining the feeling of ecstasy as one skis to the bottom of the run. No, that is not *my* idea of relaxation.

Relaxation for me means to write. To not be interrupted while my thoughts run faster than my fingers. After their first day of skiing, Judy and her daughters came back to the condominium where

I was staying and found me still content after having never ventured out into the sunlight. I slept late, I ate when I wanted to and I started writing my book – in my head. I left all my writing tablets at home thinking that I would not get to write since my husband and I were not vacationing alone. I only brought one book to read. So when Judy asked me what I did all day, I said with a grin,"nothing." I could not explain the feeling I had of doing "nothing" to Judy's daughters, when I knew the previous day, all of us were up for 21 hours but they were gone by 7:30 AM the next morning to be first on line for the lifts – "nothing" meant "everything" to me. Only Judy understood that "nothing" meant the book was already in my head from start to finish.

As I offered Judy and the girls something to eat, Judy wanted me to explain to her daughters why I was writing the book and what it was about. I hesitated a few moments. After all, I knew why I was writing and what I had to say, but I now had to explain it to Rachel, who was twelve years old, and Rebecca, who was fourteen years old. If I could explain it to them, I thought, then my story was worth telling. Rebecca and Rachel knew I had cancer in the past. I did not know if they knew I had another recurrence. It didn't seem to matter. I did not mention that the cancer was now in my bones, I told them I was writing the story of my life and then I laughed. "How boring," I said. Judy quickly chimed in, "Your life is far from boring!"

Well, I am not Barbra Streisand, though she came from Brooklyn and has a musical background, like me. I am not Oprah Winfrey, though we both know the meaning of abuse and have some of the same thoughts about it. I watched her show when she spoke of abuse. I looked at Rebecca and Rachel; they were around the same age that I was when my father's abuse came to a head. And I am not Mahatma Gandhi, who was the greatest teacher of nonviolence, though I teach English as a second language in a city school to students from various cultures where my main objective is to teach respect among all cultures. I am not even all the famous people in this world who have had breast cancer, though this is my third recurrence and I am in Stage 4. I am not Golda Meir or Martin Luther King, who had dreams for their own people, and for all of mankind, I also have my own dreams though, that my daughter will be cured of her diabetes and I will be cured of my cancer and there will be cures for all illnesses that afflict people all around the world. I have my dreams, too, for people to live without hatred, without violence, without abuse. I also want to tell my story so that my daughter will always be reminded that fear should never get in the way of anything she wants to do in life.

I want my daughter to be reminded that every day should start out as a brand new day of her life. I want her to be reminded that when you surround yourself with loving people the pain, the heartache, is made easier for you to handle. I want her to be reminded to balance work and play and to know that the pleasure you receive is in the giving. I want my daughter to know that you have to wrestle with life and appreciate every time you get to dance. Sounds corny? – So what! I have come to learn all of this as a person who feels rushed for time. If asked, "Would you live your life the same way if you were given a chance to change it?" My answer would be "Yes." Yes, because this is the life that made me who I am today. And so, for my daughter, Adrienne, my husband, Jeffrey, my family and friends and for those people who are ready to listen, I will tell my story with the hope that I can convey the feeling that life itself, with all its absorbing challenges, offers an inner serenity to people who are willing and ready to accept it. Although I will never know when I will be exiting life, I have given myself permission to accept death . . . and for that I am grateful.

DON'T TALK TO ME ABOUT RELIGION

(I HAVEN'T FIGURED IT OUT, YET)

Since this is my story, you probably want to know what my religion is and if I am a religious person. Oh come on, I know you do. When you just meet someone for the first time, don't you look at that person and think – what a cute turned up nose or see that they have blonde hair and blue eyes and you think, *"DEFINITELY – NOT JEWISH."* Well, in my case, I do not have a cute turned up nose, I have light brown eyes and dyed light brown hair. I have *earned* all those gray hairs, I just don't need to advertise them - - yet.

I was born Jewish, that means both my parents, Edythe and Max Roth, were Jewish. I was raised Jewish, which means I went to Hebrew school and played Esther in the Purim play. I married a Jewish man, Jeffrey Rothburd, which means he was born Jewish to Jewish parents, Sid and Bunny Rothburd, and he was Bar Mitzvahed. We have a daughter, Adrienne, who was born Jewish, since we are her Jewish parents and she went to Hebrew school and was Bas Mitzvahed.

So you see, we are one big happy Jewish family, *right?*

I attended an Orthodox synagogue in Canarsie (that's in Brooklyn, New York), where the men sat in the pews below and the women sat in the pews in the balcony (and here I thought that families that pray together stay together). My mother never came to synagogue for that reason. My father would attend with my maternal grandfather and I would run around with my friend (I don't recall where my sister was). We belonged to the Orthodox synagogue because it was around the corner from where we lived (definitely a reason to belong). Though my sister and I attended Hebrew school, we were never Bas Mitzvahed, most girls weren't - - well, wealthy girls were, *they* just didn't live in Canarsie. I learned to read prayer; I learned to read stories in Hebrew, I would walk to the pier with my friend Linda, whose father grew up with my mother and throw bread in the water off the Canarsie pier on the holiest day of the year, *Yom Kippur.* We had to symbolically throw away our sins; I didn't know I had any sins. I just liked looking out onto the water as I watched the seagulls swoop down to pick up the bread I had just thrown. Besides, how could I have any sins? I *always* did what I was told to do. God is good; God is one. We did not mix milk and meat, we ate "Kosher Style," everything is burned! On Passover we emptied all the food we were not allowed to eat and brought it down in boxes 25 steps to the basement. "One, Two, Eleven, Fifteen, easy, don't fall, Twenty, Twenty-five, Whew!" We changed the dishes in the house and only used special dishes for Passover. We dressed up in new outfits bought by my paternal grandmother. Though it was never spoken about, I knew I could not marry anyone other than a Jewish man (that is an unwritten Jewish law in Jewish homes).

My husband moved to Bethpage, Long Island, when he was five years old. His family wanted to get out of Brooklyn because they felt the schools were much better on Long Island. Besides, if their children had their own rooms, it would make them that much smarter (a statement my mother-in-law told my mother when I was engaged to my husband). My husband was tutored at home before he was Bar Mitzvahed, since his parents had an argument with the rabbi of their synagogue and decided to drop out of that temple. He too, grew up with that same unwritten Jewish law in Jewish homes.

Our only daughter, Adrienne, also attended Hebrew school in Dix Hills, Long Island. It was a conservative synagogue. Many times she did not want to go, I told her she had to. "Why?" she would ask,

"Because you are Jewish." I should have known then as she looked at me quizzically, it was an insufficient answer. I did *not* change dishes on Passover, we *never* walked to the water to throw away our sins, and we attended synagogue just on the high holy days, except for more days when Adrienne was Bas Mitzvahed. We did *not* light candles and have Friday night Shabbat dinners. Did I mean not to do all of this? I don't know. It seems to me that when things went wrong, we would pray to God to make them right. If things turned out okay, we thanked God. If it didn't, we would say, "You can't blame God, it wasn't His fault."

As the years passed and we went through our daughter's diagnosis of diabetes, my diagnosis of cancer, my father's and sister's deaths from cancer, the little amount of time I spent in synagogue became even less. It seemed to me, God had His own agenda - - be around in good times - - in bad times, we were left to our own devices. I was *angry* with God.

Adrienne was in college and dating a non-Jewish boy. I had no feeling about that at first because she was still young and had her whole life ahead of her. But then again, I knew many couples who married at a young age. It was time for a discussion on marriage and religion. So I began, "Adrienne, I'd like you to marry Jewish." As I recall, that was the first and last comment I was able to say during this conversation. Adrienne had her own views.

"Tell me, Mom, "She began, 'what is religion?" She gave me no time to answer. Good thing. I never sat down to figure it out on my own, like she was doing. I admired my feisty, little girl.

"In many religions," she continued, "there are many similarities. Religion stresses the importance of family and of giving. When you listen to the Rabbi, he talks about peace throughout the world. How
could we have peace throughout the world, when we don't give ourselves a chance to get to know other people from other cultures?"

By then, it did not matter to me what else Adrienne had to say. I knew she thought things through. I knew she learned to question. I knew she was brought up with a lot of love and knew how to embrace life. I knew she would do what she felt was right for her and I knew I would trust her judgment. I kissed her. End of conversation.

I know that religion binds people together; but it also separates those we might want to come to love and understand. And at my stage in life, I wanted to be accepting of everyone and anyone who added joy and growth to my life and that of my family's.

For me, religion and faith comes from within. I don't need to walk into a synagogue to pray. I don't need to walk into a synagogue to feel inner peace. I don't need to feel I haven't done anything for God. I have spent my entire life believing in the good of people and acting accordingly.

I do believe, however, in fate – that we meet certain people in our lives for certain reasons. That people say things to us that change our lives at that moment, or we remember their words later on and it forever changes the way we see things.

If God made man in his own image, as the Bible says, I can understand that because I believe very strongly in people. I am grateful for the friends I have met. I am true to myself and others. I haven't hurt anyone. I am protective of my family. I take pleasure in giving and I pray *every day* when I wake up for the health and happiness of my family and others all around the world. I say thank you *every night* before I go to sleep. If I am not religious enough for any rabbi or priest, then I have not figured out what being religious is all about. And if I have not figured it out by now . . .

I admire other religions that are more accepting of death than

Jews are. Other are taught that when you die, you go to a better place. Who *doesn't* want to be in a better place? Is living with cancer *better* than going to a better place? I haven't figured out everything about religion, so I'm not the right person to speak about it. However, if I'm given more years that I expect to live, I'll be more than happy to sit down with every leader of every synagogue, every church and every temple to figure it all out.

"DON'T BE AROUND WHEN I GET MY IRISH UP"

"Don't be around when I get my Irish up!" was said by Mrs. Patricia Lavelle, the principal of I.S. 109 in Queens, New York, where I have been a teacher for thirteen years. It was September, 1999, that Mrs. Lavelle first met with our staff as the new principal of the school. After you have seen administrators come and go, you feel you can readily size up any principal that stands before a staff of 100 teachers.

I started working at J.H.S. 109 in 1977, a year after Jeffrey graduated from Downstate Medical School. Jeffrey started his internship at *North Shore University Hospital* in Manhasset, New York, beginning July 1, 1976. We were married May 23, 1976 and we were living in subsidized apartments from North Shore Hospital. At that time, I was finishing my courses for my graduate degree in Special Education at Brooklyn College.

One day, Jeffrey admitted a patient named Sam, who had chest pains. In talking to Sam, he found out that Sam was an administrator at J.H.S. 109 and had the difficult task of recruiting substitute teaches. Jeffrey, without any hesitation, said, "Take my wife – Please!" And Sam did. When he went back to work, Sam called me his "Number 1 Sub." I loved teaching at J.H.S. 109 right away. Mr. Goodman was the principal then. A brilliant man: a tough but fair principal. I already had my BA degree in education with a license in Common Branches, which meant I was allowed to teach any course in grades K-8.

I started substitute teaching on a daily basis and then was given the long term substitute teaching position for Marylou Russell (who in later years became a principal of an elementary school).

Marylou left for maternity leave. At that time, she was teaching Sex Education. I was 26 years old and the students wanted to know when I was going to have a baby. I looked at them, held up the textbook and said, "When I read through this textbook with you, I'll know what to do and I'll have my baby." I won them over from the start. Ironically, I was then given math classes to teach after Marylou returned to work.

The same students that I substituted for in Sex Education were now in one of my math classes. Now they asked, "How come you don't have a baby yet, we read through the textbook?" I laughed - - I still laugh with my students.

I received a letter in 1979 to report to the Board of Education in Brooklyn to be appointed. Getting an appointment and receiving tenure would mean a permanent position for many years. I didn't receive it then. I tore up the letter because I knew we were moving to Maryland, where my husband was going to do a Cardiology fellowship at George Washington University Hospital in Washington, D.C. I thought we would never be back in New York again. I was wrong. I sadly left J.H.S. 109 in 1979 after having met some wonderful people who would later come into my life again and play a vital role.

I was sitting in the auditorium next to my good friend, Arleen Gomshay, along with the other members of the staff. We were listening to our new principal speak. What could she say that we had not heard before? We were seasoned teachers; nothing shocked us, nothing we heard would be new. Her name was Mrs. Patricia Lavelle, an Irish woman, in her mid 50' with blue eyes, light skin and gray hair. Her husband was Italian and they had two children (a boy and a girl). She was telling us all that, which I thought was rather sweet. She seemed like an okay lady, a very much down to earth type. I started looking around the auditorium, smiling at my colleagues. I always found humor when each principal felt that *this* year, whatever year it was, was going to be *different*. Arleen and I already had established a relationship where all we had to do was look at each other and we would become hysterical with laughter. I knew not to look at Arleen. I was feeling good that day as I did most days at J.H.S. 109. It had become my second home. It was a place I came back to after not having worked since 1980, when our daughter was born. After my first bout with cancer in 1988, I needed to return to a place that I felt safe in. I returned to J.H.S. 109 in 1990.

Mrs. Lavelle continued to speak to us and then jokingly said, "You don't want to be around when I get my Irish up." There was laughter in the auditorium, but it was not coming from me. It was then that I stared pretty long and hard at the woman who was standing in front of me: the woman who was not much older than I was. Yes, I know she was joking when she said that, but my first thought was, *How? How do you let all your anger out?* I saw my father express fits of anger, but I *never* did! If anyone had a right to "get their Irish up" then it was me! Who was this woman standing in front of me who can joke about getting angry? What right did she have and how could she be so honest about it? I could never even *talk* about being angry, let alone joke about it. It was then that I decided I liked Mrs. Lavelle.

In November 2000, I had my third recurrence of breast cancer. Scans showed it was in one of my left ribs. My cancer started out originally in my right breast. I had been seeing Dr. Kenneth Gold for twelve years already. He was a huggable, bright oncologist, who was affiliated with Good Samaritan Hospital in West Islip, NY; the same hospital that my husband was affiliated with. I was very comfortable with the doctors and nurses of Good Samaritan. I would always receive VIP treatment; but I felt that anyone would there; it was just that type of hospital.

My husband and I sat in Ken Gold's office as he told us about the treatments that were available for me at this point. I remember my first meeting with Dr. Gold in 1988. Adrienne was only eight years old and already had diabetes for four years. My energy was given *all* to her. I did not have time to dwell on my cancer and anything Dr. Gold told me to do, I did. That included a mastectomy and removal of all my lymph nodes under my arm and chemotherapy, which made me so sick and I lost my hair. But I didn't care; no child of mine was going to grow up without her mother!

The second recurrence was in 1998. Dr. Gold hugged me in his office and told me he did not plan on losing me yet. I gave him that "Let's go get 'em" smile and went for more surgery in the chest wall, took Tamoixifen and had radiation treatments.

This time, however, was different. This time, I was angry. I did not hug Dr. Gold. I sat holding on to my husband shaking as the tears flowed down my cheek, trying to listen as Ken Gold spoke of my options.

Tamoxifen failed after I was on it for two years. I was now put on another hormone, Arimidex. I would also be receiving Aredia treatments once a month. That is a two hour infusion (it was not chemotherapy), which builds up calcium in the bones and has an added bonus of alleviating pain. I had mild discomfort as though I had bruised my rib; that's when we found out; it was not a bruised rib. The infusion was to be given in Dr. Gold's office. I set up an appointment for after work. Jeffrey and I made plans to go out to dinner with friends after I got home from my treatment, which was around 6:30 in the evening. Now, stop here for a moment - - does this sound an alarm? Who in their right mind makes plans to go out to dinner after getting up at 5:30 in the morning to go to work, then go alone for a two hour treatment that I was already feeling anxious about? The reason I went alone, the reason dinner plans were made, was because everyone, yes everyone, knows that I can handle *anything!*

So off I went after work from Queens, New York, to Bay Shore, Long Island, (approximately a 45 minute ride) and sat in the waiting room until my name was called. Five minutes of waiting seemed like five hours. I was a cancer patient - - again.

"Mrs. Rothburd?" "Yes," I jumped up. I felt my legs becoming weak. *"Stop it, Allyson,"* I argued with myself silently.

The smiling nurse led me to the back of the office, where I sat in a comfortable chair and was told that someone would be right with me. I looked around at the other cancer patients. Their eyes were dead. My stomach began to turn. I tried to smile. I did a lot of smiling when I was first diagnosed, it must have never really hit me then. This time, it was hard for me to smile. I watched as other patients came back into the room.

"Hello, Mrs. Davison, How are you today?" "Well, I'm still here." Would I be saying that? I don't want to hardly be able to walk and have skin that was greenish in color and eyes that showed no life and say, "Well, I'm still here."

"OK, Allyson, this won't hurt a bit – nice veins." The nurse rested my arm on the armrest, stuck the needle in my vein and checked the bag to see that the infusion was starting.

"Great." She said, smiling at me. I glared at her. I wanted to wipe her and that smile all over the floor.

For two hours I watched people come and go. I listened to the vomitious line "How are we doing today?" *How are we doing today?* I mimicked in my mind. *Let me tell you how we are doing today,*

Miss Prissy, I want to get out of here! I am going to rip this needle out of my vein soon, if you don't get me out of here now. And then it happened. One of the patients sitting across from me receiving an infusion of chemotherapy had a reaction to it. She could not breathe. I watched in horror how she was struggling. I watched nurses surround her, speaking in calm quite tones as they injected her with epinephrine. In my horror I thought *"you bastard, why didn't you just let her go – bastards!"* When the woman was breathing easily again, she caught my eye. I started to cry. I was crying for her and for all of us sitting there.

My two hours were up. "See you next month." Miss Prissy nurse said. I glared again, *"like hell you will, I thought."*

I ran to my car feeling a little weak and a little out of breath, but I got there. I used the clicker to unlock the car door. I swung open the door, got inside, slammed the door shut and banged on the wheel screaming, *"You fucking bastard!"* The tears were now running all over my face. I tried to wipe them with my sleeve, but they would not stop. I put the key in the ignition, turned it on and took off like a bat out of hell. I saw traffic lights, but didn't pay attention to what color they were. The highway from the south shore to the north shore where I lived became the Indianapolis 500. I swerved in and out of cars. I nearly missed the divider and saw at a quick glance the speedometer was past eighty mile per hour. Where was a cop when you needed one? I was *dangerous* to myself and to the other drivers, but who was thinking? I was too busy cursing my life and that of my family.

Why were my legs glued to the floor as I watched in horror as my father held my sister's neck under the bathtub faucet as she was bent backward on the floor over the bathtub? I screamed while swerving the car. *I remember the look my sister gave me, as she broke free. Did she think I didn't want to help her? Did she know I couldn't? I was thirteen. I could not move. My sister was sixteen and used to it. Fuck you, fuck you all you bastards!*

God! Oh God! Are you listening?! Why is my sister dead? Because she was too good a person? Huh - - you only take the good ones, well, don't worry, you won't be seeing me! Brenda was a better person that I was and you better leave my daughter alone! You touch my daughter, one complication from diabetes and I will come after you, that's right, I will come after you! What are you going to do? Give me CANCER!?

Somehow I got home in one piece. With my face soaked from the tears, I ran into the house. Jeffrey was not home yet. I ran upstairs, dropping my coat along the way. I thought I would get into a shower but stopped at the top of the stairs and turned and went into my study. My desk and the top of the bookshelves were filled with books and photographs. With one arm, I cleared everything off my desk and in a rage, turned and used the same left arm to clear the top of the bookshelves. Everything came crashing down. I held my hands to my head and stood looking at the mess on the floor. I was sobbing like I have never sobbed before. After a few moments, I just stood in the middle of the mess and picked up a picture of my sister. "I'm sorry," I whispered. I then looked at the mess around me and thought, *"You stupid jerk, who do you think is going to clean up this fucking mess!*

I walked out of the room leaving the mess I made behind me and headed for my bedroom. I undressed, dropped my clothes on the floor and walked into the shower, letting the hot water fall all over my body. The water felt good; it calmed me. I stepped out of the shower and stared into the mirror. "Okay," I whispered, "Everything will be okay." I got dressed and went into my study to clean it up when suddenly I heard the door open downstairs. It was Jeffrey.

"Ready, honey?" - - he shouted, "We have a 6:30 reservation."

I went downstairs, wrapped my arms around Jeffrey and said, "I don't know how to tell you this, but I think I'm part Irish." Jeffrey kissed me and said, "Whatever makes you happy, hon, whatever makes you happy."

We met our friends for dinner; all the men in the group were doctors at Good Samaritan Hospital: Bernie Nash, Larry Engelberg, and Faizur Chowdhury. Jeffrey and the rest of them all decided that I was *not* to have treatment at Dr. Gold's office again. I was going to receive home care treatment from then on. I did not argue.

That night as I lied down next to Jeffrey completely exhausted, with a faint smile, I quietly said aloud, "Thank you Mrs. Lavelle."

"IT'S NOT HOW LONG YOU LIVE THAT'S IMPORTANT,

IT'S HOW YOU LIVE YOUR LIFE THAT COUNTS"

It was 1988, the year of my first bout with cancer when I dropped Adrienne off at the Dix Hills temple for Hebrew school. I walked into the synagogue that one particular day. At the same time, Susan Ross was dropping off her son, Ben, who was the same age as Adrienne, eight years old. I knew Susan, but we were not friends then; we had some friends in common though. I knew Susan had multiple sclerosis after the birth of her only son. Susan sat down on the couch in the lobby of the synagogue. Though I was not working at the time, I saved my errands for when Adrienne was in Hebrew school. It gave me two hours.

As I started to walk out the door, something made me turn around to look at Susan. I wondered why she did not just drop Ben off and go home. I approached her and the words just flew out of my mouth, "Why are you still here?" I said, even surprising myself. Susan didn't seem to mind. "It's become harder for me to drive back and forth for Ben, so I just stay here until he's done."

It didn't take me a second to forget about my errands and suggest that she come home with me since my house was very close to the synagogue. "Come on, I'll make you a fresh cup of coffee," I said.

Susan's eyes lit up. After that we spent many hours talking while the kids were in Hebrew school. Susan was a Columbia graduate who studied music. She gave piano lessons to many of the children in the neighborhood. I had been a student at Hartt

College of Music studying violin. We had a lot in common. We both loved life. We were both fighting our illnesses so that they would not interfere with the lives of our families. We both knew how to laugh and we made each other laugh. We also both planned on being around to watch our children grow up.

It was on a Sunday when our mutual friends, Anna and Bennett Berman, invited a group of people to their home for a pool party.

Susan and I sat in the shade as we watched our husbands and children play in the pool. We were like two little school children giggling away. Then Susan became serious. She was telling me that she had to give up teaching piano because she was having trouble moving her fingers. She told me she needed to exercise more. I didn't know what she meant by exercising more. What could she do to help her fingers move better?

The next day I received a call – *Susan was dead.* She had drowned while exercising in her own backyard pool. She was only thirty-four years old. My knees buckled from under me. My thoughts ran wild. *How could this be? We were going to watch our children grow up! Remember?*

There were crowds of people at Susan's funeral. I stood next to my husband motionless. When the Rabbi got up to speak, I thought, *go ahead Rabbi, say something that will make sense out of all this chaos.*
Go ahead and explain to an eight year old boy that his mother is never coming back. Go ahead Rabbi, try it!

Then the Rabbi, who I never met, began to speak. "It's not how long you live that's important, "he began, "it's how you live your life that counts." You could hear a pin drop as he continued to speak. *Okay, I thought, okay, I can accept that.* I think of Susan as I watch her son grow up into a fine young gentleman and I think of the Rabbis words very often.

ONCE YOU HIT BOTTOM
THE ONLY WAY TO GO IS UP

In December 2000, Adrienne went out to Breckenridge, Colorado to work as a ski instructor during her winter college break. I was nervous for her. It was the first time she was skiing without her father while on the insulin pump. Adrienne had been on insulin injections up until she started her third year of college; so this was her first vacation with the insulin pump.

The insulin pump looks like a beeper. A small catheter is inserted into the skin with tubing attached. The insulin flows through the tubing and into her body. Adrienne calculates the amount of carbohydrates she eats and programs it into the pump. It gives her a lot of freedom of when to eat and when not to instead of three or four daily injections. She changes the infusion set every three days.

Adrienne didn't want the insulin pump before, but didn't have much choice since her hemoglobin A1c's were getting out of control over a period of three to four months. She agreed to it three weeks before she had to return to Hamilton College in Clinton, New York (a five hour drive from our home).

The insulin pump takes more than three weeks to adjust to. As in many cases, it needed to be fine tuned. Adrienne insisted on going back to school whether she was comfortable with it or not. She knew she was a fast learner. I knew it could cost her her life.

During the past summers, Adrienne worked in her father's office. She loved the field of medicine, which was a complete turnaround from when she just entered college. Her words then were, "I want nothing to do with science ever again." At Hamilton she thought she would major in English, but after working for my husband and riding the ambulance with an Emergency Medical Technician ("EMT"), Adrienne decided she would start taking all science courses and apply to medical school. It seemed the right path for her to go, since hospitals and needles were part of her life from age four.

In her second year of college, she started training to be an EMT. She filled her schedule with laboratory sciences. She was happy when she worked with a professor who was doing a study on turtles and diabetes.

During the summer before her junior year, Adrienne worked hard to learn everything about the insulin pump. One morning, my husband and I were awakened by a scream of "Help!" We both ran downstairs to find Adrienne becoming hypoglycemic. She was in the midst of changing her infusion set when she bottomed out. My husband ran for the emergency kit of glucagon and orange juice, as I held her head and tried to get her to take sips of the drink. My body immediately calmed. I remembered the time when Adrienne was five years old and had a seizure from hypoglycemia. I had to hold her then too. I spoke softly to her then as I did now. I watched her body stop shaking as she drank the juice as the injection of glucagon took effect. When Adrienne came to, she was upset. She knew if this happened when she was alone, help might come too late. It was not a good time for me to speak to her about taking a semester off from school. She had two weeks to go.

I waited two days to speak to her. "Adrienne, I'm very proud of you, "I began. "I know you don't shy away from challenges, but don't you think that it wouldn't be such a bad idea if you took a semester off from school where you would have time to adjust to the pump?" Adrienne stopped what she was doing and looked at me. I continued, "Perhaps you can go to one of the local colleges for the semester and then go back to Hamilton." I thought she might agree with me for one fleeting moment. I was wrong, very wrong.

Adrienne began to speak in very slow, controlled sentences. "Everything you taught me, is it all lies now?" I knew where she was headed. I need to sit down. "You taught me *never* to give up. You taught me that my diabetes should *never* interfere with anything I want to do in life. Were you lying to me when you said that? Were they just words to you or did you really mean it?" Her words pierced through my body.

"No, Adrienne, they were not lies, I meant every word I said." As I said that, I looked at Adrienne and thought how far we had come. Anything and everything Adrienne set out to do, she did. She went at things with such vigor, with such love, with such an embracing of what life has to offer that my next statement to her was "Do you need anything before you go back to school?" Adrienne shook her head no and turned and walked out the door.

She was twenty years old. For every setback, she had twice the amount of strength to move forward. By age twenty, she was good at just about everything she touched. In high school, she loved to sing and would do the harmony parts with her friends in cantata (a select group of choral students). She won the music award and was given the all- around student award when she graduated. She was on the varsity tennis team, but did not pursue it in college. She played piano, was a member of the honor society and had friends from all walks of life. She *knew* how to listen to people.

Adrienne loved mountains and down to earth people. By age twenty, she had her head screwed on straight. By age twenty, I knew I had to straighten out or else. Right after Adrienne got home from Breckenridge, she left the next day for an interview at Hartford Hospital in Connecticut. She interviewed for a program to take part in medical seminars and shadow different doctors as well for the coming summer. She also had an opportunity to do research at Hamilton. All of this sounded great . . . except the mention of Hartford Hospital brought back painful memories for me.

I was twenty years old in 1971, attending Hartt College of Music in West Hartford, Connecticut. I was at the end of my sophomore year and living in the dormitory. The first year, the dorms were full and I would end up living in a woman's house, who rented her rooms out to college students. It was good for me to be there. The dorm life for me was a disaster. Everything was becoming disastrous. My grades were falling. I knew a few people; I dated, but did not feel close enough to anyone. One night, my roommate was out for the evening, I had nowhere to go. I looked around the room and saw a bottle of aspirin on my roommate's shelf. What did I have to lose, I thought. I'm not good at anything I do. I did not want to live the life I had in Brooklyn and I figured no one would miss me anyway. I really did not want to die, but I did not want to live either, so I grabbed the bottle of aspirin off the shelf and started swallowing a few pills. After about eight or nine I got scared. *No. I DID NOT WANT TO DIE.* No one was around. My dorm suite was empty. I panicked and called for security. They came quickly and brought me in on a stretcher to Hartford Hospital, a city hospital that seemed dreary even back then. I was drowsy but kept my wits about me. I was alone and I didn't trust anyone. My instinct to be on my guard kicked in.

A team of nurses surrounded me. Before I could say anything, the head nurse already had enough information about me and decided to handle things her way. She asked me how many pills I had taken. Meekly, without looking at her, I said, "I don't know." Obviously, an answer she did not want to hear. She came close to my face and in an instant slapped me so hard, I thought she broke my jaw. I was shocked. Is this how they treat you in a hospital? I held my hand to my face. "I'll ask you again, how many pills did you take?" She said sternly. "Six, maybe eight, ten, I don't know" I said hesitantly. "You don't know?" I had not heard of *One Flew Over the Cuckoo's Nest* yet, but if ever there was a nurse Ratchid, she was it!

"How would you like it if we pumped your stomach? It's not a pleasant procedure." "Don't pump my stomach, " my voice grew stronger. I stared straight at her this time. "this is what I am going to do with
you," she said matter of factly. "I'm going to keep you here overnight. I will give you something that will make you sleep. Then, in the morning, you are going to go back to your school and you are going to straighten yourself out." With that, she left and the other nurses took over. They were gentler, but again, they did not stop her.

In the morning, I don't remember how I got back to my dorm. I sat on my bed alone and said aloud to no one in particular, "NEVER, EVER, AGAIN WILL I ALLOW MYSELF TO STOOP SO LOW."

I was twenty and my life had just begun.

HALLELUJAH

In elementary school at P.S. 115, in Canarsie, teachers called me Sarah Bernhardt. I was the one telling jokes, playing the violin and always entertaining. For our school play of Camelot, I played the part of Mordred. I wore black tights over my skinny legs with a long, yellow vest that my mother had sewn for me. Being skinny and flat, I was perfect for a knight in shining armor. My hair was covered by a black hood so that only my face showed.

After the play, a parent came up to my teacher and wanted to know who that cute, little boy was who played Mordred. "I'm not a boy!" I cried. "No you're not," replied my teacher in her warm soothing manner. "But don't you understand? It means that you played your part very well!" No, I did not understand, I just knew that my teacher's skirt was soaked as I sobbed into it and used it as a handkerchief!

At Bildersee Junior High School, I had a choice of joining the chorus or orchestra in 1965. I didn't care for the orchestra leader at all. He demanded respect, a trait that I was too familiar with. I did, however, hold the highest respect for Mr. Presti, the choral leader. He was an older Italian gentleman who said few words and was able to draw out exquisite musical tones from his students. I opted to join the chorus. The orchestra leader let me know that he was not pleased with my decision. I compromised by staying after school to help him tune the instruments and rehearse with the orchestra. During the day, I rehearsed with the chorus.

In chorus, I was part of a group of some very talented students. Tina was among them. She sight read and played the piano for Mr. Presti as we all took our places in our respective voice sections.

Tina also was the only one who had a car at the time that we were of driving age – a Camaro. On Friday nights, a group of us would hop into Tina's car and drive to Flatbush, Brooklyn, to hang out on the coolest corner, looking *cool*. Every Friday evening, we stood there thinking we were *cool*, never realizing no one else thought we looked cool. After two hours of coolness, we would hop back into Tina's car and go home.

I loved chorus and I loved Mr. Presti. As the night of the music concert approached, I only wanted to sing. Mr. Presti advised me to play with the orchestra and when it came time for Handel's Hallelujah Chorus, which was to be jointly performed by the chorus and orchestra, I was to take my place on stage with the chorus. I agreed to this.

As I sat in the first chair of the orchestra, I watched as the auditorium began to fill up with families and staff. I saw my parents and sister walk in. The auditorium was full; the concert began. The orchestra leader motioned for me to sound my A string. The others followed in unison. We played a few pieces. I kept my eye on both the music and the conductor. Did he realize how much I loathed him?

Then the chorus came on stage. I immediately straightened up. I listened to the sounds as I watched as everyone kept their eyes on Mr. Presti. He had a very warm, loving presence about him – yet, he was a master of perfection.

The time had come. The Hallelujah Chorus was about to be performed. I was still seated with the orchestra. The orchestra leader raised his baton and looked at me with the slyest smile. My eyes darted back and forth from the chorus to the orchestra leader. I felt my heart race. He seemed to take delight in all this. Mr. Presti had his baton raised also, but just as he was about to begin the downbeat, he looked over his shoulder and saw me staring at him.

What could he do now? I thought. Just then, Mr. Presti lowered his baton to his side and motioned for me to come take my place with the chorus. I jumped up and took my place on stage. I wanted to hug Mr. Presti right then and there, but thought it best if I just sang out "Hallelujah!"

HOW DO YOU GET TO CARNEGIE HALL?

THE SAME WAY YOU GET TO HARTT COLLEGE OF MUSIC

We all know the old joke – *How do you get to Carnegie Hall? Practice – practice-practice.* Well. I did get to play at Carnegie Hall (with the Brooklyn Borough Wide Orchestra) and I did get to Hartt College of Music - - but I didn't practice. Not in the true sense of the word. When you practice, you are supposed to analyze each section and work on parts you are uncomfortable with. I never really did that. I would go from beginning to end, skipping over the hard parts because I didn't like the way it sounded. Besides, during the week when I came home from school, I did my homework first, which left little time to practice since I was not allowed to play the violin after 6:00 in the evening when my father came home from work. When my father came home, he wanted silence. He wanted to eat dinner and spend the rest of the evening watching television. My practicing was just noise to him.

My sister Brenda, played the piano and I played the violin. We both attended the same music school. Do you think that at any point in our lives we played duets together? *Heart and Soul* does not count. The answer is *NEVER.* We never played a duet together! In a duet, you need to intertwine with each other, you need to listen to each other, and you need to create a balance between you and the person with whom you are playing. We never did, in our music.

Every Saturday we attended Third Street Music School in lower Manhattan, New York. Over the years, the music school offered us dance, theory, private lesson, orchestra and most importantly, it offered us an escape from our home life. At this time, I was taking dance lessons while Brenda took dance and piano.

Our annual concerts were held at Town Hall. My sister and I had to travel by train alone. At the time, my father owned a hair salon in Brooklyn (a job that lasted only a few years) and he needed my mother to work in the shop with him on Saturdays.

My mother instilled in us the rules to follow on the one hour subway ride from Canarsie to Third Street and Second Avenue. I was eight years old and Brenda was eleven years old. "Stay together, don't talk to strangers, and don't look at anyone in the eye." We listened. We always did.

The train was coming. I loved the sounds that the trains made. I stood close to the line where the train pulls in as I leaned over feeling the breeze. Suddenly my sister yanked me back, "Stop that, stupid!" Stupid and Allyson were synonymous. We got onto the train as other people pushed and shoved. My sister held me by my coat collar. She found two seats and swirled me around until I fell into one of them. I wanted to look at the person sitting across from me, but I remembered the rule – "Don't look at anyone in the eye." So I just watched while my feet swung back and forth all the way until we reached Manhattan. My sister, however, paid attention to the train stops. She was older and therefore smarter than I was. We were going to get off at 14th Street and First Avenue, even though there was an easier way to go. However, 14th Street had more people around and seemed safer. We could either walk south eleven blocks to Third Street and go one block west to Second Avenue or we could ride the bus down on Second Avenue. We usually walked the distance.

The train came to a halt, a lot of people stood up as Brenda and I were getting up. Somehow we got separated. I panicked. I could not see my sister and I was being pushed around. Suddenly, I felt a hand grab mine – it was Brenda's. She pulled me off the train just as the doors slammed shut.

"Are you okay?" she said as she straightened up my collar. I nodded my head, "yes." Brenda smiled at me and as she said, "Come on, let's go," without calling me stupid. I knew she loved me.

I spent a total of ten years at Third Street Music School. Six of those years with one violin teacher, Eva Kovach Roberts. Eva was a Hungarian woman who came to live in the United States in 1950. She lived eleven years prior to that in Brazil, having to escape the Nazi persecution. She and her husband, Alex, lived on the Upper East Side in Manhattan. He was a man who admired his wife and shared her love of music. Though I was only eleven years old when I met Eva, I knew that admiration and sharing of interests was at the heart of a good marriage. These traits would always stay foremost in my mind. The Roberts never had children, and when Alex died before the age of 65, he left Eva alone for many years after that. I still visit her on a regular basis. We have dinner together and spend hours enjoying each other's company.

Eva was a very proper lady. Her shoes matched her handbag and her clothes were tailored to perfection. She was highly intelligent and spoke six languages fluently. I was a little shy with her at first. My lessons with her consisted of an hour of scales, etudes and a classical piece of music. Eva also conducted the junior orchestra of which I was a member. "One, Two, Three, Four," she would count. I was usually off a beat. "No, No, try it again – you have to practice!"

As I grew older and college was beginning to factor in with my plans, I had no idea what I wanted to do or what school I wanted to attend. The guidance counselor at Canarsie High School suggested that I go to Hartt College of Music, in West Hartford, Connecticut. After all, I always played first chair in the orchestra and I was among three other students in the school to have won the Lincoln Center Award. This award allowed us to attend many performances held at Lincoln Center. I was also voted *Class Musician* for our high school yearbook.

My mother thought it was a good idea. I had no thoughts about it and Eva was dead set against it. So much so, that she dropped me as her student in my senior year. I was devastated. The year before college she *dropped* me! I was given another teacher.

Auditions for Hartt College of Music lasted about five hours. Sight reading, sight singing, written theory tests, interview, and performance tests. I came out to the waiting room where my mother was and proclaimed "I made it, I know I did!" And I did. It was an honor to make one of the top conservatories in the country! Eva couldn't believe it. I was a student who enjoyed music. I didn't eat, breathe, or taste it every day the way you are supposed to if you attend a music conservatory. A harsh lesson that I was about to learn.

I spent two and a half years at the music school and the other half year taking more academic courses at the University. It was a time of the hippie generation. A time when I met people who were very involved with the whole movement. I was not involved. The 1970's brought a lot of drugs and free love – *not* my style. I just liked listening to people who had different views than I did.

One of the good experiences I had in college was that I always loved to write. I wrote for the school newspaper. I took advanced creative writing courses. At one point, I challenged the professor not to mark certain papers that the class had to hand in.

"It's a creative piece." I said. "There's no right or wrong here. Just put a check mark to show that we handed in the work. Don't mark it." I even went so far as to say, "If you must put a grade on my paper, then fail me, I don't want my work graded." The professor looked at me and listened as the class remained silent. When we got back our papers, there was just a check mark on top.

"Do you feel we're all against you, Allyson?" I was sitting with my mother around a huge oblong table with the Chairman of the Music Education Department, who was also my conducting professor. The rest of the panel were professors who I never had and who didn't know me. I hesitated in answering because I knew every single question required a thoughtful, definitive answer.

"Well," I began, "I don't feel you're here to help me. How come this panel is filled with professors who don't know me? Why don't you call in Miss Mende?" Miss Mende was my piano teacher. I enjoyed her class. "With all due respect," I continued, "I don't find it fair that any of you are here, except for my conducting professor."

Hartt had a policy that if your grades were declining they would call you and your parents in for a conference before they decided to either throw you out or put you on probation. A humiliating procedure. I was not one of those students who blamed their teachers for their grades. I did accept responsibility for my own grades. I knew in my mind this professor had to justify me being brought in to the panel. I challenged him.

"Our final was based on conducting the Hallelujah Chorus, wasn't it?" I said with a long hard stare. I know that piece inside and out. I conducted it *perfectly* (I knew Mr. Presti would have been proud). The Chairman said nothing in response. He continued, as did the others in their rehearsed sermon. In the end, they decided to let me continue at Hartt ... on probation.

I went home and wrote a poem about taking clay and molding it to make me look like them. I hated them, I hated anyone associated with music, I hated my violin, and I hated the fact that that's what I learned from Hartt College of Music.

I closed my violin case and never opened it again until fifteen years later when my daughter asked if she could take violin lessons.

BACK TO BASICS . . .

BROOKLYN, THAT IS

"You're really going to have to work hard, Allyson."
"I know, Judd, I know."

In 1972, I was in Warwick, New York, in the home of Gladys and Judd Dunn. Gladys grew up with my mother in Canarsie and Judd, who was married to Gladys, drove my mother and father to the hospital when my sister was born in 1948. Judd was also the Dean of Admissions at Brooklyn College. He was reviewing my transcript from Hartt College and though he did not say it at the time, he knew that after three years of college I had to practically start all over again.

"Are you up for the challenge?" Judd asked me.

"I'm ready as I will ever be," I answered. This time I was determined to be in a field that I knew I was suited for and do well!

"You will have to go to both summer sessions," Judd was saying. "Perhaps you can take some music exams instead of sitting through the courses. That'll help you out"

"Whatever it takes, Judd. I'm ready!"

Not every person is ready to go from high school to college. Not every person knows what they want to do right away when they enter college. My husband always knew though. He knew that he would attend Rutgers University in New Jersey as a chemistry major and go on to medical school. I wasn't so lucky at first, but the important thing was that when I was ready to make my deci-

BACK TO BASICS . . .

sion, it wasn't too late and I made the right decision for me. I loved teaching. I loved kids. It's never too late to find something that you love to do!

I moved back home, which really wasn't terrible since I did own a car that my maternal grandparents bought for me. This was after they learned I was riding on the back of a motorcycle while at Hartt. I was free to go as I pleased and never took advantage of staying out late.

Who would I stay out late with anyway? My friends were either engaged or had boyfriends. I wasn't engaged, nor did I have a boyfriend.

I entered a program at Brooklyn College, which was to be the first performance based program in education; meaning we did a lot of student teaching in different schools and then had seminars back at the college. It was a terrific program where we could really get our feet wet and know what it was like to prepare lessons and stand in front of a class of thirty or so students. We taught in areas of East New York where they warned us to walk in groups when we entered and left the school.

By the second day, I had already learned every student's name in the class. I also could identify the students who needed more attention. When I saw one of the students write in a mirror image, I knew that I
had to learn every facet of teaching so that I could work with all students, not just your average or gifted student. I decided that my graduate work would be in Special Education.

I went to the Music Chairman of Brooklyn College to see what credits she would accept from my transcript. "Do you think Hartt College is a better school that our music program here at Brooklyn College?" she demanded to know.

"Of course not," I knew how to play her game. "I don't have to do anything for you." "I know that, "I said. *You're a typical music administrator,* I thought to myself, *you don't have to do anything for anyone – just destroy them* ."I'll let you take a few exams to get your credits, I assure you, and they won't be easy." "Thank you," I said with a smile as I walked out.

"Bitch," I said aloud after I closed her door. I passed the exams with flying colors.

I enjoyed every moment at Brooklyn College. I met a small group of friends and we traded stories of all the students we worked with. In one of our seminars, the professor asked us to write a short
composition on what we perceived the educational environment was like for these students in the ghetto. Everyone started to open their notebooks. I sat with mine closed. The professor started to do some work at the desk for a few moments and then looked up and saw me with my notebook closed.

"Finished, Allyson?" she asked. "Yes," I replied. "Are you sure?" "I'm sure." "Would you like to come up here and share what you wrote with the rest of the class?" She knew I didn't write anything.

I got up and faced the class. What my professor didn't know was that even before she gave us this assignment, I had already thought about the students in the schools living in a neighborhood that was worse than mine. I had written something at home and kept it in my head. Instead of a composition, I started snapping my finger and keeping the beat with my foot as the class joined me in my rhythmic composition.

I began:

"Books . . . Read

Paper . . . Write
Pens . . . Pencils
(pp)   Out of Sight
Desk . . . Chair
Student . . . That's me!
(cresc)   Teacher – This is where
I don't want to be

Now one and one are two
(mf)   And two and two make four
And four minus two
Is also two
(f)   So c'mon in
We got plenty to do . . .

(mf)   In school
My name is Johnny
(mp)   What is yours?
I got brothers
And a house without doors
My father works
(mf)   My Mom's out at night
My grandma's home
But – Oh what a sight

I go to school
To learn to read
(mp)   I go to school
They say
That's what ya need
I like to write
But my gramma is paw

My teacher rips it up
(f)   As I go cryin' out the door
I don't understand it

       Please explain it
       I don't understand it

(f)   My mind can't frame it
       I talk fine at home
       I'm well understood

       I come to school
       And my teacher says
(mp)   "No Good"
(pp)   Books . . . Read
         Paper . . . Write
         Pens, Pencils
(accel pp) – Watch-
         I'm Out of Sight."

The professor and my classmates applauded.

During the time that I was taking courses at Brooklyn College, my mother was majoring in Art Education. I graduated with a Bachelor of Arts in Elementary Education in January, 1974 (a semester after I was supposed to graduate). My mother graduated in June of 1974. The commencement ceremony for both classes were held in June. I did not partake in my own graduation, but watched proudly as I sat with my father and grandparent as my mother received her diploma with the other graduates.

WHITE LIES AND CAVIAR DREAMS

My parents, sister and I had our reservations on Amtrak. We were leaving New York to go to Greenville, South Carolina. A one day trip to visit the Pandolfi's. The Pandolfi's were an Italian family with talented children. They were a very close knit family who made music very much a part of their lives.

Unlike our house in Canarsie, the Pandolfi's lived in a one family house. Their home was sparsely furnished, which made the rooms seem larger than they actually were. We spent good times at the Pandolfi's home; always listening to Barbara and Pam on the violin, Emil on the piano. Anne let me hold a three-quarter size violin. I placed it under my chin very carefully, like I had seen Barbara and Pam do. Then Barbara showed me how to hold the bow. She slid the bow between my thumb and middle finger as my other fingers naturally wrapped around the top of the bow with my pinky finger resting on top. She placed the bow between the bridge and the fingerboard on the A string. "Bring the bow up and down in a figure eight movement," Barbara said as she showed me.

I mimicked her bowing as I played an open A string. Emil, Barbara and Pam started to play a concerto. I was now playing with experienced musicians!

Anne Pandolfi allowed me to keep the three-quarter size violin and suggested to my mother that I take violin lessons at Third Street Music School in New York. I did. It was 1961 and I was 10 years old. The Pandolfi's soon moved to Greenville, South Carolina.

We entered the train and found our seats. "Sit down girls," my mother said as she pointed to our seats. "And remember what I told you to tell the conductor." I didn't want to tell the conductor what my mother told me to say. When he came around in his blue uniform with a pleasant smile to check our tickets, I leaned closer to my sister. Let her tell the conductor that I was nine years old instead of my real age of eleven.

"Tickets, tickets, please." "Hello girls." "Hello," my sister replied. The conductor looked at the tickets, then looked at me. With a smile he said, "How old are you?" I looked at my sister. There was a moment of silence. "She's nine," my sister piped in.

The conductor laughed to himself, as though to say, *here's another family trying to beat the system.* He moved along without saying anything, and then he started up again, "tickets, tickets please."

I turned to my mother mortified. "Why did I have to lie about my age? You know I'm not nine." "You didn't really lie," my mother responded. "You told a white lie."

"What's that?" I asked. "A white lie is telling someone something that is not the whole truth, but it doesn't hurt anyone."

I never heard of that. I didn't know lies came in colors. I didn't know our whole life was like living a white lie. All I knew at that moment was that I was eleven years old and not a day younger.

The severe beating with my father's belt strap aimed at my sister began when Brenda was eleven years old. I was eight. Without any warning, my sister would be dragged off into the bedroom that we shared and beaten until my father was through. My father would come out of the bedroom, put his belt back on in front of me and then continue to do whatever he was doing.

I got up and went into the bedroom to find my sister lying face down on her bed with her head buried in her pillow. I *never* heard her cry loudly; I *never* heard her scream either. After each beating, she would lie quietly with the pillow muffling her sounds.

I would go over to her side of the room and sit at the edge of her bed. She felt me near her and would kick her feet signaling me to get off the bed. I went to the opposite side of the room where my bed was. I liked the location of it. It was parallel to the ledge of the windows that took up three-quarters of the wall. They were casement windows with no screens. We lived in a two family, semi-attached house on the second floor. At night, I would sit on my bed and stare out into the blackened sky.

"Please God," I would say, "Please don't let him hurt Brenda ever again."

As I grew older, I would dream of the day when I would live in a big house and have a wonderful husband and a lot of kids, where we would all be happy.

At young ages, my sister and I learned that white lies didn't hurt anyone. . . just us. I didn't know at the time how Brenda got through the rough times. I found out after she died. I, however, always held on to my caviar dreams.

A TREE GROWS IN BROOKLYN
- IN MY BACKYARD

A Tree Grows in Brooklyn, by Betty Smith was one of my favorite books. At the time, though, I related to the tree . . . not the symbolism relating to the growth of Frances. My backyard had one tree that, at times, had to be cut back when it hovered over our next door neighbor's yard. Why couldn't they just leave it alone? I used to look at that one lovely tree and think that one day I would have a backyard full of trees!

Our backyard extended ninety feet in length. A factor my mother was very proud of. "We have the biggest backyard in Canarsie," she would proclaim with such pride. "Yes, Mom, but we have a house half the size of all the newer homes."

Mom had a way of defending our home, like a soldier defends his country. When my father walked one block heading for the post office and was mugged during the day, my mother exclaimed, "He should have walked the other way!" When he wanted to move to Florida after he retired as a Trade Specialist for the Federal Government, my mother wouldn't give in.

"How could we move to Florida when we have a one fare zone!" A one fare zone meant that you could get on the bus and pay one fare and be taken right into the train station without having to pay again.

When my father died, my mother moved to Florida. So much for the "big" yard and one fare zone!

My mother grew up in Canarsie. Now, Canarsie is in Florida.

Growing up in Brooklyn did have its advantages. We could walk everywhere for whatever we needed: the movies, pizza, ice cream, and your friend's house. Sometimes you didn't even have to leave your own block to find kids to play with. That's because of "THE STOOP." The stoop served its purpose on hot summer nights. Who had air conditioning? We didn't even have screens on our windows. How did my mother know that living on the second floor of a two family house my sister wouldn't throw me out of the bedroom window?

If someone were to ask me what I remember most about my block, I would have to say the two telephone poles, the mailbox and the Italian kids that I played with.

The two telephone poles, which were about thirty feet apart from each other, were very instrumental in my learning how to ride a twenty four inch bicycle at the age of five. The bicycle was really bought for my sister, but she had no interest in it. I, on the other hand, would never concede to the fact that if you crash into one pole and go flying off the bike and land so that the bike is now on top of you and you have scrape marks that are starting to bleed on both knees and elbow, that this would ever happen if you head towards the other telephone pole. All I can say now is that I am so grateful there were only two poles. Upon remembering my father's expression at the time, he was very relieved as well.

Most people believe that a mailbox is used for sending mail. That is correct! However, did you know that when you travel at a very fast speed on roller skates (the skates that you slipped your shoe on and tightened the front clasps with your skate key that you wore around your neck) and you misjudge turning the corner- it is the mailbox that makes contact with your chest. You think that every rib is your body is broken before you go down hard on your bottom with your feet outstretched in a V in front of you. As I sat dazed for five minutes with my friends' mouths hanging open, I very slowly got up and realized that my ribs were still intact. I was just in pain. Therefore, the only thing to do was to take off again as my friends followed behind. The mailbox, as it turned out, probably saved me from oncoming traffic on a very busy street.

Canarsie had a very large Jewish and Italian population. My block was ninety percent Italian, We would play handball against the side wall of the corner grocery store and stoop ball together. We would also play hit the penny, double Dutch or just sit and talk. There was no difference until I walked into my friends' houses and saw the crosses with Jesus Christ hanging in every room. It made me feel a little uncomfortable. Uncomfortable because I was the only Jew. I would divert my eyes and pretend I didn't notice anything hanging on the wall.

When I awoke in my hospital room from having a mastectomy in 1988, I found myself looking up. On the wall above my head was a crucifix with Jesus Christ. With my eyes fixated on the cross, I was so grateful to be alive.

MY SOUTHERN EDUCATION – YOU'RE NOT IN BROOKLYN ANYMORE, ALLYSON

"Remember, Anne will meet you when you get to Greenville. Here, take some money" The trip from the Greyhound Bus terminal in New York City to Greenville, South Carolina, was an eighteen hour ride. It was 1964. I was thirteen years old and travelling by myself. I walked to the middle of the bus, slid into the seat by the window and pressed my nose to the glass. As the bus started to move, I smiled and waved goodbye to my mother.

After a few hours, the bus pulled into a rest stop. The passengers got off. I watched as they carefully took a step down – no one my age.

If I get off, I thought, I might not find my way back. There were so many buses and they all looked alike to me. I decided to stay on. When everyone returned, we started on the road again. After more hours of riding, the bus stopped again at another rest stop. By now, I was feeling a little weak and hungry. I looked at my watch. It had been thirteen hours since we left New York. Sleeping was out of the question. I was not going to sleep with strangers around me. I knew I had to get off the bus this time though. If I didn't eat, I figured, I would die and if I died, my mom would feel awful about sending me alone to Greenville. I walked to the front of the bus and took one, the two steps down. After that, I didn't recall what happened. I awoke in the arms of a nurse, who had my head cradled in her lap.

"What happened?" I did not want to cry. "You fainted," the soft voice of the nurse reassured me that I was going to be all right. "Are you travelling with anyone?" she asked while keeping me still. "No," I replied, as my eyes darted around at all the people who were surrounding me. Someone must have told them to back away and give me room, as I felt a distance between the crowd and myself. "But I'll be meeting my family's friend when I get to Greenville," I quickly chimed in.

I had noticed an ambulance parked nearby and I did not want the nurse putting me in it. I pushed myself up, trying to show her that I was much stronger now and could continue traveling. As I stood up, I started to fall backward. The nurse grabbed me and as the tears swelled up in my eyes, I told her I just wanted to get back on the bus. She smiled at me and stroked my hair as she said, "Don't worry, you'll get to Greenville."

I was given something to eat and drink and then helped back on the bus. I kept my eyes down as the bus driver closed the doors and started the bus going again. I was sorry for holding everyone up.

It was so good to see Anne Pandolfi waiting for me. As I jumped off the step of the bus, I ran towards Anne, who gave me a whole body squeeze. I liked Anne, she was always laughing! As she drove me up her block, I noticed how pretty everything looked. There was no congestion of cars or buses or noise from car horns. The homes weren't attached.

It was so easy to feel at home in the Pandolfi house. I was shown upstairs to what would be my room for the next few weeks. I ran and sat on the bed, feeling the cover for its softness and thought, *wouldn't it be great if I lived here forever?*

During the early 1960's, Brenda spent her summers in North Carolina performing with well known actors in summer stock. Pam and Barbara Pandolfi were part of the orchestra when Brenda went to visit them. With her huge, dark, expressive eyes, the director of *Bye-Bye Birdie* thought Brenda would be perfect to stand silently on stage looking sad as *Put on a Happy Face* was being sung to her. The director did not know how right he really was. Brenda was perfect for the part!

I quickly became friends with the Pandolfi's next door neighbor, Lynn. Though Lynn was my sister's age, she acted more like my age. She loved running around, always joking about something and keeping active, just like me. Where Lynn went, I went too. I sent a letter home to my parents:

Dear Mom and Dad,

Today I went with Lynn to her uncle's farm. Lynn is old enough to drive a jeep, so she showed me how. It was pretty bumpy at first, but I caught on real quick. By next week, Lynn said I'll be able to drive the jeep all by myself.

Love,

Allyson

There were other letters I sent home that were real shockers:

Dear Mom and Dad,

Would you believe it – Lynn and I can't go swimming anymore at the Community Pool. We'd go swimming practically every day, but Lynn said we can't go anymore because it's now open to the Negroes.

Love,

Allyson

After that letter, my mother thought it best that I return home.

My mother had saved all my letter throughout the years. When she moved out of Brooklyn, she showed me that letter. I read my letter over and over again in shame and thought, *why wasn't I smarter then?* I started to remember other experiences during the summer of 1964.

Lynn's mother needed to be driven to the garage in town where her car was being fixed. Lynn was going with her mom and asked me to go along for the ride. Another neighbor and friend of Lynn's mother, Ernestine, was going too. Ernestine was the epitome of a real Southern Belle. Her porcelain white skin and blue eyes sparkled even under the brim of her hat that she wore in her ever so lady like manner. The driver from the garage pulled up in front of Lynn's house. He was a black man. Lynn, her mother, and Ernestine all started getting into the back of the car. I opened the front passenger side door and was just about to step into the front seat when Lynn's mother spoke in an admonishing tone, "Allyson, sit in the back with us." I stopped my leg in midstream and looked at the driver, the empty seat in front and then I looked at Lynn, her mother and Ernestine.

"There's no room in the back to sit," Why couldn't they figure that out? "I'll sit up front," I said as I put my leg down. "I said, sit here, Allyson," Lynn's mother's voice was more demanding now.

"Allyson," Ernestine started to say. "No thank you." I interrupted, turning to sit in the front passenger seat. The driver waited until I shut the door. We drove in silence, When we got out, I thanked him. I thought it was the polite thing to do. No one else said a word.

That evening, Lynn's mother told Lynn to tell me I was never to do that again. Lynn told me and we both rolled our eyes.

The summer of 1964 came and went. In retrospect, it was one of the most significant years in our nation's history. President Johnson signed the Civil Rights act as the Reverend Dr. Martin Luther

King, Jr. looked on.

The signing of the bill, however, did not end the racial violence. The search for the three civil rights workers in Mississippi, Michael Schwerner, James Chaney and Andrew Goodman, continued.

Just the year before, a powerful blast killed four young black girls, Denise McNair, Carole Robertson, Addie MacCollins and Cynthia Wesley, in the Sixteenth Street Baptist Church in Birmingham, Alabama. Four decades later, Thomas Blanton, Jr. an ex-Klansman, stood trial for the bombing.

In 1964, the Imperial Wizard, Shelton boasted about the Klan's membership in such states as Alabama, Louisiana, the Carolinas, Tennessee, Georgia, Mississippi, and California.

When I think back to my summer spent running barefoot in Greenville, I'm still confused with the thought that I never fully recognized the racial tension of the South. At the end of the summer of 1964, I returned home to concrete sidewalks and small, enclosed rooms. In 1969, Ernestine was found murdered in her home.

According to the article in the Greenville newspaper, an autopsy showed that there was evidence showing suffocation and that respiration stoppage was the cause of death.

I never asked if the man responsible for Ernestine's death was white or black.

"YOUR SISTER SUFFERED ENOUGH"
I Had No Idea What This Meant

"Clean the bathroom, your sister suffered enough. Clean the hall, your sister suffered enough. Vacuum, dust – your sister suffered enough!"

I cleaned the bathroom and the hall. I vacuumed and I dusted because my sister suffered enough- I had no idea what that meant nor did I ever question why I cleaned the house and Brenda did not.

Brenda was born on January 13, 1948 with a head of dark, black hair. My mother would always say that when people would look into the carriage, they would say, "Don't worry, she'll grow up pretty."

When I was born on May 14, 1951, my mother would say that people would look into the carriage and exclaim, "Now this one is a beautiful baby!" When I looked through the photograph albums after my sister's death, I can assure you that it was my sister who was born the beautiful baby.

The Salk vaccine for polio was not available in 1948 and many people suffered the effects of polio. My mother fell victim to it first. She spent seven months away in a hospital in West Haverstraw. My sister was less than a year old at the time. My father had to take care of my sister and go to work. A task that was too overwhelming for him, even with the help of my grandparents and aunt and uncle. With no money for medical expenses, my mother was considered a "guinea pig" for the vaccine trials.

My sister, soon after my mother's diagnosis, began to suffer the painful effects of polio as well. My mother carried the guilt of Brenda's diagnosis throughout her life. Thus the expression "your sister suffered enough" was a constant in our house.

The result of polio left my mother's left side weak. My sister was left with a slight limp. My mother's work in pottery yields outstanding results. My sister was head choreographer of dance during her senior high school year at Tilden for the class competitions. She also studied dance at Julliard Preparatory School of Music in Manhattan. Later on, my mother wrote out a check for a few thousand dollars to the March of Dimes, as a donation. The same amount that it cost the hospital for my mother's stay.

I was strong and healthy. Though, Brenda and I were brought up in the same house, we were treated very differently.

"Eat everything on your plate!" my father screamed at us as he looked across at my mother's vacant seat at the table. "Your mother should be here doing this, where is she?" he said as he continued to dole out the mashed potatoes and green peas and put it on our plates.

I often wondered why he asked where my mother was, since she never hid anything from him. Maybe her train was stuck in the tunnel. I *never* worried where she was. "I'm not really hungry." I said. I was never really hungry. Dinner time, the time that should be the most pleasant, the time I imagined my friends sitting down with their families and laughing and telling jokes or discussing how their day in school went, was the worst time in our house. My father was always tired when he came home from work and he demanded silence at the dinner table. Never did he ask us how our day was. Never did I care about his.

"You're not hungry?" he bellowed. I realized I made a big mistake and it was already too late for me to take back my words. Brenda would fall victim to his wrath all because I wasn't hungry.

With one arm, my father knocked my plate of canned green peas, mashed potatoes and two baby lamb chops onto the floor. As I jumped from my seat, he had already dragged Brenda by her hair into the bedroom for a beating. I picked up the peas, one by one, so that I could focus on the food and not on what was happening around me. I then picked up the two baby lamb chops and scrapped some of the mashed potatoes with my fork from the floor back onto my plate. I sat at the table silently, trying to control my shivering until my father came back to the table, without Brenda, and sat down. I kept my eyes on my plate, as we both ate in silence – until both our plates were completely empty.

I learned to tune out my father's screaming and would turn away in disgust as he kicked his feet while sitting on the floor. I always, however, remained sensitive to my sister's outbursts. Sometimes, not often, she would physically lash out at me when she was overly frustrated. I let her dig her nails into my hand. At times, I touch the small scar and only think good thoughts of my sister. On the way to the hospital to get stitches near my eye, after my sister lashed out with a hairbrush to my face, I knew I would come home and tell her it was alright, that she didn't hurt me. I was willing to pay the price of being physically hurt by her to take away a drop of my sister's pain and anger.

When Brenda was first diagnosed with cancer in 1990, it was my father who helped care for her along with other members of the family. He would cry and when he lie dying of cancer of the bladder in 1993, he only asked for her forgiveness.

During the last few months that I spent with my sister, after I finished work on Friday, I would fly out of Kennedy Airport to Miami Airport where my brother-in-law, Marc, would drive me to their home. I would stay until Sunday evening when I would return home. I would head straight into Brenda's bedroom ready to tell her a new joke I had just heard. By this time, she comprehended only half of the joke. The cancer had spread to her brain. I would hold her up and try to help her walk a few steps until she grew tired. I would rub her back until she fell asleep, remembering when she would rub mine to practice one of her skills as a physical therapist.

Brenda often used me to practice skills she wanted to acquire. Lucky for me, they had nothing to do with dissections – that she saved for school. She graduated New York University as a physical therapist and was certified in neuro-developmental treatment in Florida, where she worked at the University of Miami Mailman Center for Child Development. She was a board member of the Miami Choral Society and expressed herself beautifully through writing.

Before Brenda died at age forty-eight, she wrote a poem about my father and her in heaven. It was a beautiful poem. I knew that her life ended peacefully for her and that her years of suffering were over.

When her husband of 24 years asked me if I wanted to take anything of Brenda's, I said, "yes." I only wanted her doll that she had named Patty. The rest could go to her children, Maia and Ben. Patty was a thirty-six inch doll that brought so much joy to Brenda when she was young. I took Patty home from Florida with me right after my sister's funeral. I made sure to wrap the doll carefully and put it in my suitcase as I traveled home to New York. Patty, I was convinced, knew and saw everything. She was with Brenda as a little girl, and she sat next to Brenda's bed on her own little bench as Brenda lie dying.

Patty now sits on my bookshelf in my study looking out the window, wearing an outfit I bought at the Gap for her. When I look at Patty,

I'm reminded of my days spent with my sister as a child and as an adult. I remember Brenda saying to me when she moved out of the house and into her own apartment on the upper west side of Manhattan at age twenty, that although she suffered physical abuse, I had suffered mental abuse and that she was very sorry for that. I remember not knowing what to say, I was just grateful to be enjoying her company in her own place.

My sister's diary was also given to me. I have read it hundreds of times over and I understood that that was how she managed to cope.

THE BRANCHES KEEP FALLING
OFF OUR FAMILY TREE

In 1979, while Jeffrey was doing his fellowship in Cardiology at George Washington University Hospital, I was teaching at Parkland Junior High School in Montgomery County. We were living in Silver Spring, Maryland. I suppose I should have been happy to find a teaching job in Special Education, but it was a year when I felt like a non-entity. I had just left New York, my home, my friends, my teaching job and my security. I needed to take a license exam to teach out of state. Maryland's test for teaching consisted of two hundred questions: one hundred in English and the other hundred in math. I got two wrong on the English part and one wrong in math – I thought the exam was too easy and remembered the exam we had to take in New York for our license to teach. Questions were asked for all subject areas and essays were given to test our grammatical skills to see how concisely we could write on any given topic. I passed. I had a job.

Montgomery County in Maryland reminded me many times that I was still in the South. I remember walking into Washington, D.C in the Administrator's office to apply for a teaching job. I walked into an office entirely made up of black people ready to hand in my resume. As I walked up to a woman at the front desk, I said, very self-assuredly, "I need a teaching job and would like to work in this district."

"My dear young lady," the kind woman replied as she looked around the office, my eyes following hers, "Don't leave your resume here, go to Montgomery County." She smiled. I understood her message. I wanted to say . . . "But I'm from New York." I did not think it would have mattered. I thanked her and headed for Montgomery County.

My special education class was small. All white students. It was mostly an all white staff. Everyone was friendly, but I didn't have friends. I missed home. When I asked my student what they did on vacation, they told me "hunt'n."

"Hunt'n?" I went over the concept in my mind. People hunt for food, but "hunt'n" for pleasure, to kill innocent, harmless animals for one's own satisfaction, was appalling to me.

I knew I wasn't going to last too long at Parkland. I didn't. I didn't know that I was pregnant in September and therefore left before the school year ended in May, when Adrienne was born.

Adrienne, of course, to me, was the most beautiful baby I had ever seen. After needing a Caesarian section, I found Adrienne to be very patient and gentle with me. Personality traits that still, for the most part, remain with her today. Summers in Maryland are hotter than summers in New York. While Jeffrey went off to work, I sat outside our apartment building on a bench keeping cool while rocking Adrienne in the carriage. Another woman around my parents' age, sat next to me. We struck up a conversation. She was waiting for her thirteen year old daughter to come home from a friend's house. She told me she had two older sons. One my age and one three years older than me. A second marriage, I thought. I was wrong. As we spoke, I mentioned I was looking for an occasional baby sitter.

"How about my daughter?" she said waving as her daughter come running towards us. "Hi," I said. "Hi," her young cute daughter replied. "I can't, she's very young," I said to this perfect stranger. Somehow though, I knew I could trust this woman sitting next to me, who I had never met before, or so I thought.

"How about you? Would you help me out every once in a while?" *I KNOW NO ONE* must have been written across my forehead.

"Sure," this sweet stranger replied. Her name was Lorraine. She lived upstairs with her husband and daughter and had grandchildren living in West Germany, where her son and daughter in law were stationed during part of his military career.

Lorraine loved plants and moving furniture. We became quick friends. She came with me to the supermarket. She came with me to the clothing store. She watered my plants and thought it best if I put my couch on the other side of the room. Jeffrey drew the line – plant's okay – but no moving furniture! Six months had gone by since I got to know Lorraine. Then one day she told me she was going to West Germany for three weeks to visit her son, daughter in law and grandchildren. Her husband and daughter would remain home. I told her not to worry, I would look after them. I knew I could cook a dynamite lasagna, my Italian neighbor taught me how to make it while I was dating Jeffrey. "The way to a man's heart is through his . . . " "I know, I know," I would laugh with my neighbor.

When Lorraine returned from West Germany, she came downstairs to our apartment to thank me for keeping an eye on her family while she was away. "Where's Adrienne?" she asked. "Sleeping," I responded with a tired sigh.

"Oh, but I have pictures of her to show you." Jeffrey chimed in proudly. Without hesitation, he put the photo album on Lorraine's lap. She started to laugh, understanding what a proud parent acts like. As Lorraine flipped through the photo album, her smile started to diminish. *What could be wrong, I thought.*

Lorraine continued flipping the pages, back and forth, then back and forth again, until she finally glared at me. "I know these people," she pointed to my mother and father. "They are my parents," I felt I needed to quickly defend them, even though I knew I never introduced Lorraine to them. How did she . . . before I could finish my thought, Lorraine asked me, "Did you know Irving

Mattis?"

"Of course, I did," I replied immediately and without thinking added, 'He was my grandfather." "Your grandfather?" Lorraine could hardly get the word out. By the hesitation in her voice, it clued me in to add, "my father's step father, my step grandfather."

"Did he let you call him grandfather?" "Yes, yes, of course," I said, my head began to swirl. What was she getting at and who was she. I wanted to know. Lorraine continue to speak, "I am Lorraine Mattis, Irving's daughter," as she hesitated, then said, "I hated your grandmother!" Lorraine put the photo album down and stood up. "Isn't it ironic? Here I am babysitting for your grand-mother's great grandchild; I can't, I won't!"

Jeffrey and I were speechless. Lorraine continued, "I knew your father, he was always kind to me when I saw him, the little that I saw of him. I met your mother too, she was okay, but your grand-mother," Lorraine shook her head with disgust, "I'm sorry, Ally-son, it's not you, you are sweet, but I cannot help you anymore, you understand. I will let my daughter help you when you need it, but I have to go now."

I did not stop the woman who sewed curtains for Adrienne's room. I let her walk out of the door. As fast as she entered my life, that's how fast she exited it.

I knew the story. I just never knew that it was Lorraine Mattis who my grandmother had hurt so badly by living with her father, as her mother lie dying of cancer. It was Irving who went along with my grandmother and didn't allow Lorraine's sons to call him grandfather. I had answered quickly, I don't
recall calling Irving grandfather, but I said I did, *why did I do that?* My paternal grandmother was married to William Roth before she met Irving Mattis. William was a phantom to me. I met him once.

"Come on, Allyson, get in the car," my father said to me when I was ten. "Where are we going," I asked. "I'm taking you to meet your grandfather. .. My father?" I knew that Irving was really not my father's father, but he was the only one I saw when I went to visit my grandmother in her apartment in Brooklyn. No one ever really spoke about my real grandfather, except to tell me that he had served in the
Navy, was never around for my grandmother and was "hospital-ized" for many years somewhere.

"Your grandmother is coming with us. Now listen carefully," my father spoke seriously, "your grandfather doesn't recognize your grandmother any more so I'll just tell him she's a friend of ours, understand?" "Yes," I said, knowing full well it made no sense to me. I thought *how could my grandfather not know his own wife but know his son?* My father kept looking at me until I assured him that I wouldn't say anything.

The drive was long. I had no idea where we were going. When my father parked the car, my grandfather was already waiting for us. I did not know what to expect since no one ever showed me a picture of him. I walked slowly on the grounds of the hospital, smelling the freshly cut grass. I remember wondering if he knew I was his granddaughter. My father said, "Hello," and then intro-duced my grandmother as a friend of the family. William bowed his head a little to my grandmother and softly replied, "Hello," My father then began to introduce me. "And this is Allyson, my daughter."

I smiled up at this handsome man. He returned the smile and then put out one finger on his hand to me. I immediately held on to it and walked slowly away with him, not even looking back to see if my father and
grandmother were following. No word was spoken between us, just a feeling of serenity as I walked for the first and last time with

my grandfather.

"We have to go now," I heard my father call in the distance after only twenty minutes. "Didn't we just get here?" I questioned as my father moved closer to me. He gave no reply. I knew I had to go, though I didn't want to. I let go of my grandfather's finger and quietly said, "Good-bye." I don't recall if he answered, but I do recall that he turned and walked toward the tall building. I stood watching him until I could no longer see where he went.

"Why did he put out his finger for me to hold and not his whole hand?" I asked. "Because he wanted to be careful not to squeeze your hand too tightly, he didn't want to hurt you," my father answered. "He would never hurt me." I said in a strong tone looking straight at my father. My father had no other comment as I got back into the car for the long ride home.

A few years later, at age fifty-nine, my grandfather died. The memory that I have of him I will always cherish, as he was ever so gentle with me, in spite of what was said about him.

My paternal grandmother was a fun loving woman, an "American," as opposed to my maternal grandparents who were immigrants. My sister and I would visit my grandmother on a weekly basis. There was always something good baking in the oven in her small kitchen. Her living room chairs and couch were covered in plastic.

"Ouch." I would clench my teeth and squirm as I tried to unglue my thighs from the plastic on hot summer days.

My grandmother loved showing off her new possessions, no matter what they were. She was living a good life with Irving. "Now, here's my new lingerie." She would hold up her new bras, underwear and slips as though they were the Queen's jewels. I would hide behind my sister in embarrassment and giggle as I pushed my sister to the forefront to get a closer look. Brenda would push back at me, but really had nowhere to go.

When parents tell their children to wear clean underwear in case a car hits them- my grandmother was actually teaching us that your underclothes should be as nice as your outerwear. There was no difference, except that my grandmother was always ahead of her time, whether we were ready for it or not.

"Come on Bubby," I would pull her to come into our bedroom to sing to us so that we could fall asleep. I would jump into my bed as my sister got into hers. "Sit on my bed, Bubby."

My grandmother loved to sing. She tucked me under my covers as she sat next to me and began to move her body to the upbeat rhythm as she sang, "I'm gonna come down and get ya in a taxi, honey. Better be ready by a half past eight. Now baby, don't be late... "

"Now how am I supposed to go to sleep when you sing a song like that?" I would giggle. My grandmother would continue singing a few more bars, and then she kissed me and Brenda goodnight.

Lorraine had her own thoughts about my grandmother, but she was my grandmother and I loved her, she was fun to be around. While I was in college, my grandmother died at the age of seventy-two. When Irving died, Lorraine and her husband were at his funeral. That is where I had seen Lorraine for the first time so many years ago.

My maternal grandparents were from Russia. They were first cousins who escaped the pogroms of Europe when they were eighteen years hold. They managed to survive by always having a trade. . . and diamonds. My grandfather was a barber and my grandmother was a seamstress. When they arrived in America on the Byron, a ship that landed at Ellis Island, their name was changed from Charnovetsky to Charnow. They already had one baby in tow with two more to be born. With their hard work, quick wit, and innate social skills, they managed to prosper and own the largest hair salon in Canarsie.

It was in my grandparents' store that I learned more about the interaction of people and life than anywhere else. Some people were good listeners, others good talkers. Some people were charged the price that it said on the chart for a haircut, some weren't; some rules are made to be broken, some aren't. Sometimes if you work hard, it pays off – more tips; sometimes you work hard and you get nothing for it. It was in my grandparents' store that I knew a hot meal waited for me during the school week when we were allowed to go home for lunch. It was there that I also stayed after school until my parents returned home from work at 6:00 in the evening.

"Let's read together, Big Mommy," the name we used since my grandmother thought she was too young to be a grandmother, when the eldest of her grandchildren, my sister, was born. My mother was "the mommy," thus, the name "Big Mommy" evolved. Even when we were grown, we were still calling her "Big Mommy."

"I don't know how to read," my grandmother replied with her eyes cast downward. At nine years old, I never knew that people did not know how to read – more shocking, I didn't know my grandmother did not know how to read. My instinct of protection kicked in. When you love someone, you don't want them to feel bad. "We can do something else," I said, as I watched her lift her eyes and smile at me.

My grandmother never let on to her clients that she could not read. If anyone handed her a letter to show off that their grandchild had written to them, I was quick to say, "can I read it aloud?" Being cute can get you places, being cute made me feel I saved her from embarrassment.

My grandmother died when I had my first bout with cancer in 1988. My grandfather died a few years after; I'm convinced of a broken heart.

My father was not always bad. He loved baseball and he was a very dedicated son. He grew up in an abusive home, an explanation my mother tried to convince me of when I told her I didn't want to hear what a saint he was after his death. He was a follower, not a leader. He switched jobs often. When I was four and Brenda was seven, we left Brooklyn for a year so that my father could get work. We lived in a restricted area, so I was told. "No Jews Allowed." We lived on Kent Road in Wappinger Falls. The area was beautiful; our rented house was small. People thought my father was Italian with his dark, wavy hair and large dark eyes. He wanted them to believe that, therefore, no friends were to come to our home. My sister

attended school. She was to take the bus to school and come straight home by bus. I entertained myself with the kitten that I had found and regrettably was responsible for his death. I held him too long so that when I let go, he ran and was hit by a car. I fed the birds as I sat on the caretaker, Ludwig's shoulders. Ludwig would wheel me in the wheelbarrow down to the lake where my father would take me fishing or in the winter, ice skating. My mother would sit and paint the scenery. Though I remember this time from photographs of me playing with my sister, I was told this was the year that I hardly spoke. It was the year that I could not even pronounce my own name and told people that my name was Mary.

"Why Mary?" my mother asked. I opened my hand and showed her the small statues I had found of Jesus and Mary. My mother wanted to return to Brooklyn, so we did.

I remember my father being very good to us until I was eight and Brenda was eleven. Then the beatings started. Before that, it was my father who took us sleigh riding and made snowmen with us or paddled in the canoe with us during our two weeks in Lake George every summer. What made him snap? Why did he refuse to get help? My mother explained that my father was never the same after she had contracted polio. Also, he was sent to a psychiatrist once but refused to go back again. I realize that in the fifties psychiatry was not a topic to be spoken about, an antithesis to the way it is today. *"Oh, sorry, can't do lunch, I have my session with my therapist. See you later perhaps."*

What I don't understand and never will is if you have a family who you love and you know something is very wrong, wouldn't you want to do anything in the world to protect your family, even if that meant protection from you? If seeking help will protect your family then why not seek help?

My father settled into a job working for the federal government in the Department of Commerce. He held a high school diploma and never wanted to obtain any degree higher than that. Though he and my mother loved to dance, he loved his television even more. He was a gentleman to strangers and neighbors. He was good to his grandchildren; he took out his frustration on his family. From when he was fifty on, I always heard him say, "What's the use, I'm going to die by the time I turn seventy." My father retired at age sixty-five when he believed that was his time to travel. He made one trip to Italy, which brought back his happiest moments of when he was in the army during World War II. He attended my daughter's Bas Mitzvah and died six months later from cancer of the bladder at age seventy in 1993. At his funeral, my mother told the Rabbi that he was the best husband and father in the world, "a saint of a man." As the Rabbi listened intently, I sat quietly and stared straight, looking at nothing in particular.

Oscar Wilde once said, "No great artist ever sees things as they really are. If he did, he would cease to be an artist." My mother was an artist in the truest sense of the word.

Defense mechanisms work wonders. There's one problem, when using a defense mechanism to protect yourself, you don't realize that you are shutting other people out who need you for their protection.

My mother was never lazy. She was good in math and kept all the bills and balanced the checkbook. She sewed all our clothing including coats and rarely had to work with a sewing pattern. She volunteered for the March of Dimes for many years and was president of the Parent Teacher Association when I was in elementary school. She was the head leader of the Girl Scouts in our neighborhood. She could draw, paint, and make pottery, having studied at Greenwich House of Pottery and Arts/Student League in New York City. She holds a Masters in Art Education; and she has friends from all walks of life and all ages. My mother survived her bout with cancer of the kidney, exclaiming "I had the best kind of cancer to have, no chemotherapy!"

"No comment."

So how did I know not to go to her when I had a problem? Why did my kindergarten teacher say, "Please, Mrs. Roth, spend more time with your daughter than with the PTA."

My report card from my first grade teacher had the question written on it that said, "Does Allyson have a library card?" My mother's answer, "Of course she does!" My mother was there, but she wasn't.

She said she gave me music lessons to keep me off the streets. I was happy on the streets playing with the kids on the block. My mother was caught between making a life for herself to survive and seeing to

it that my sister and I were safe. With a limited income, my mother tried to do the best she could for us. However, actions speak louder than words with children. When you are trying to do the best you can for your family, but act helpless when it comes to protection of your children, you do not score any brownie points!

"Where were you when Brenda was getting beaten up?" I once asked my mother, as Brenda was struggling to stay alive with metastatic breast cancer. "I don't know. If I wasn't there, how do I know if it really happened?" My mother thought she could get away with that answer.

"I was there and, unfortunately, so was Brenda. You believe what you want." I turned away in disgust.

It was only after Brenda's death that my mother admitted that she knew of the severe beating Brenda received. She told me how my father wouldn't go for help. I explained to her that a mother's job is to protect her children.

Right after my father died, my mother made a new life for herself by selling the house in Brooklyn and moving to Florida where she had many friends. She still does her pottery.

"I DID IT MY WAY"

In 1988, I was preparing to have a mastectomy and walked into the ambulatory unit at Good Samaritan Hospital. Dorothy Hunt was the head nurse of the unit. I did not know her but she knew Jeffrey, and liked him. As much as I respect caring, intelligent doctors, I hold the utmost respect for nurse. They make you feel better, even when you are not aware of it.

Dorothy grabbed my hand, introduced herself to me and pulled me into the cubicle behind the curtain. "Now listen to me," she said as she started unbuttoning her blouse. *What was she doing? Wasn't I the patient?* I didn't know where to look.

"You're very lucky," Dorothy continued. "Now they do a modified radical mastectomy, that means you will be able to have reconstructive surgery." *Reconstruction! Isn't that what everyone is doing in their kitchens?* I didn't know what to think. Dorothy was on her last button. "Look!" I looked. "When I had it done, it was a radical mastectomy. Everything was removed." Dorothy's chest was shockingly flat. Didn't Dorothy know I didn't have a strong stomach. I didn't say thank you, after all, I didn't ask to be pulled into the small cubicle. I just shook my head and pulled open the curtain just enough for me to get out, leaving Dorothy alone to button up her blouse.

Shock, reality. Okay, so I am lucky.

After sponge baths lasting five days, I was able to take a real shower in the hospital. I never looked at my chest after the mastectomy though I let the doctors and nurses poke and prod at my body as I would glance around at the walls, the floor or look at all the plants and flowers from numerous well wishers that filled my room. My first shower in five days, I was excited.

"Can you handle it yourself?" the nurse asked as she walked me up to the door for my shower. "Sure," I said, smiling while thanking her. "I'll be back in ten minutes to check on you, okay?" "Okay." It never dawned on me how I would feel when I would sponge my chest down and feel my breast missing. It never dawned on me that there was a full length mirror in the room of the shower. I stood in front of it as I untied my bathrobe and slowly removed it. Now, for the first time, I was staring at what I thought was another person.

"That's you, Allyson," I whispered to myself. Within seconds I found myself grabbing on to the wall as I felt my knees buckled from underneath. I pulled myself up, clenched my teeth and reminded myself that I was alive. Alive . . . I would be going home the next day so that my daughter wouldn't have to visit me in the hospital. I was alive . . . I stepped into the shower holding my face up so that the water from the showerhead would wash away my tears.

I was home the day before Mother's Day; the time of year that we would always celebrate since it was my thirty-seventh birthday on May 14th. Adrienne's eighth birthday was on May 18th and our twelfth wedding anniversary was on May 23rd. And celebrate we did!

I started chemotherapy treatment at Dr. Gold's office. The office manager was my next door neighbor and one of the nurses was a good friend of a friend of mine, so I felt very comfortable. The rest of the staff was also so very kind and caring. They made vomiting after each treatment bearable.

I sat in the waiting room trying to make eye contact with a few of the patients sitting there waiting for their turn for the poison to enter their bodies. Some glanced at me with a quick smile then turned their eyes downward. Some thumbed through magazines not reading anything in particular. One man smiled at me and kept contact with my eyes. His name was Mr. Wick. He sat with his wife during each treatment. We became comrades in battle. I knew very little about Mr. Wick, an elderly gentleman with a nice face. We would chat about the weather, how nice everyone was here and how he liked my painted cap that my daughter made for me when I started losing my hair. Months of unimportant conversations went by with Mr. Wick as we sat in the waiting room until our names were called. Five months into treatment, I walked into the waiting room one day and didn't see Mr. Wick. Where was my buddy, my partner in crime?

One of the nurses called me over to her and whispered, "Allyson," she began getting my full attention, "Mr. Wick is in that room. The doctor just told him that they can't do anything for him anymore and his wife isn't here, she fell and broke her hip. Go in there and talk to him."

I was stunned. What do you mean the doctor can't do anything for him. They have to, and they must! Mr. Wick is such a good man, a kind man. I walked into the room where Mr. Wick sat with his head down."Hi, my friend," I said as Mr. Wick lifted his head and tried hard to smile. "Hey, listen, you've come this far, you're not giving up, are you?"

Mr. Wick just listened. "Ah, what do the doctors know, you think the doctors know everything? They can't or else they wouldn't be human!" I was on a roll now, my chemotherapy partner couldn't leave me coming to the office and walking in and not finding him.

"You think," Mr. Wick began. "I think you have a shot at this, don't give up, please."

I had to leave him as the nurses held off calling my name as long as they could. "Bye, Mr. Wick, I expect to see you around." I touched the brim of my painter's hat. Mr. Wick waved and with no sparkle left in his eyes he said goodbye. He died ten days later. I never knew until I read his large obituary in the newspaper that he was a well known political leader of Suffolk County.

When you are young and just starting out as a cancer patient, you can't comprehend that an end is in sight. At least, I didn't. I gave Mr. Wick false hope but in retrospect he probably was glad that I still had a lot of fight in me, he knew better for himself though.

———————

"Dorothy Hunt is in the hospital, Allyson," Jeffrey said. "What for?" I wanted to know. "She's dying, go see her," Jeffrey said flatly.

I visited Dorothy a few years after the unbuttoning blouse scene. I knocked on the door to the small room where Dorothy sat upon her hospital bed, waving her arms to greet me into the room that was her sanctuary. I looked around. "Nice flowers, Dorothy." "Aren't' they beautiful," she said too cheerfully. I dared not ask how she was feeling. What do you say to a dying woman after you have come to know cancer very well. I looked at Dorothy and thought back to the day I met her. She was right. I was able to have reconstructive surgery. Not that it mattered to my husband. He would take me with or without a breast. It was me who wanted to feel "whole" again.

"Listen, Allyson," Dorothy began. *Oh no, another reality shock from Dorothy Hunt, I thought.* "I'm dying and this is the best way to go, my way." I looked at her infusion, not knowing what was being dripped into her veins. I could not speak. I didn't have to. Dorothy could speak for anyone and everyone.

"This is really great, I get to see everyone I want to see and say goodbye. I got all my papers in order." My stomach was getting queasy. I didn't want to throw up all over Dorothy. I didn't know what was getting to me, the thought of her dying of colon cancer, the way she was so matter-of-fact about it and so in control, or the hospital smell that I couldn't figure out existed or not.

I told Dorothy I would always remember her, who wouldn't. There's a section now in Good Samaritan Hospital named for her. I didn't understand at all how a person could be so calm when facing death, something I have come to terms with only now, thirteen years after my initial diagnosis.

I quietly said goodbye as she touched my hand. When I left her room, I felt I no longer had to say strong so I went home, threw up and cried.

Cancer, as horrendous as it may seem, gets you to put things in perspective. When you think you are appreciative of your surroundings, your appreciation increases three-fold when faced with a fatal illness. You seek out the people who understand the meaning of life.

In 1998, I had my second recurrence. I thought for sure after ten years, I was free and clear of the disease. It was now in my chest wall and more surgery was needed. My implant was removed as well as chest muscle. If Dorothy were alive, I would have shown her that we were twins now.

Radiation, not chemotherapy and *Tamoxifen,* a hormonal treatment that promised everlasting hop, was prescribed for me. Instead of receiving radiation at Ken Gold's office, I was going for treatment at Good Samaritan Hospital.

The waiting room was filled. I sat next to an elderly woman who was attached to a portable oxygen tank. Her husband sat next to her. "Hi," I said. The woman just looked at me, her husband responded with a hello. I noticed that around the oxygen tank, held by a strap, was a small stuffed toy.

"He's cute," I said pointing to it. "Does he have a name?" "No." The woman responded breathlessly. Though she was frail looking, she reminded me of someone who, at one time, could take on the world. I learned their name was Rothe.

"Do you want to name him?" Mrs. Rothe said glaring at me. "Yeah, I would. Can we call him George?" I don't know why I said George; it just seemed the right name to give this creature that seemed to want to break free.

As time went on, I looked forward to seeing the Rothe's while coming for my treatment. My feisty friend fought hard to breathe. I was on a scheduled amount of radiation treatments.

"You know, you ought to pipe in music in each room," I told the doctor, "it relaxes people." As I lay on the table, I would listen to only Emil Pandolfi's CD's. Emil was now a well known musician. Before I knew it, everyone was asking me for a tape of his to play in all the rooms. I was finishing up my last treatment of radiation when Mrs. Rothe said, "Wait, I have something to give you." She reached down and pulled George out from under the strap and handed it to me.

"But you need him," I didn't want to take it. "Take him and remember me," Mrs. Rothe said. I did. George sits right on my desk in my study so that I can smile when I think of the tough woman who wasn't so tough at all. Before she died, I had sent her a replacement for George so that she had something soft to stroke when she grew anxious; the reason George was there in the first place.

Dorothy Hunt, Mr. Wick, and Mrs. Rothe were just a few of the patients who came into my life and left. They are never really gone though; I still see their faces clearly.

Having to go through another recurrence two years after Tamoxifen failed, I just say to my husband, "Dorothy Hunt, I want to go like Dorothy Hunt." What I didn't understand about her years ago, I understood now. It's about control. I was advised by someone who told me to let Adrienne do as much as she could to regain control of her life when she was diagnosed with diabetes; just as Dorothy was in control when she was dying. Control is something we all want to have in our lives. I'm grateful to have met such wonderful people. They taught me more than I could ever imagine in the short time I came to know them.

ONE SMALL STEP FOR MANKIND
ONE GIANT LEAP FOR ME

In 1995, five years after I had returned to I.S. 109, my friend and colleague, Lorenza Colletti, lost her son, Marc, in a drowning accident. He was in his twenties. She and her husband, Joe, were devastated to say the least. Lorenza was a friend who I had met in the late seventies along with Arleen Gomshay when I just started teaching.

We would have lunch together every day and trade stories about school, students, movies, books, and jokes. We would laugh so hard in the teacher's room, that the teacher next door would beg us to tone it down so she could teach her class. When Marc died, I attended his funeral along with many members of our staff. After taking some time off from school, Lorenza returned to work, still distraught. Some days she would sit at the table for lunch with us; some days she would stay in her room alone with the lights off.

On one such day I went to her. "Lorenza, is there anything I can do for you?" I said feeling so helpless even as the words came out of my mouth. Lorenza looked at me and with piercing words began, "You! What do you know? Your life is so perfect!" With that said, she walked away from me. I was left standing not sure if I heard her correctly. Lorenza, my friend, would never talk to me like that. I knew she was in pain. I now knew she didn't trust me to help her. I was always taught "not to hang out your dirty laundry." No one really knew my true thoughts, my true feelings, no one really knew me, because I didn't let them and I wasn't ready to, with or without Lorena's piercing words.

Sometime later, Lorenza, Arleen and I were in a restaurant in New York City before attending a Broadway show. It was a dimly lit restaurant. We were just talking in general as we always did. The topic of discipline came up and how parents handle certain situations. Suddenly, I felt my eyes swell; it was like someone took a key and opened me up so that all my thoughts, feelings and words came pouring out. Lorenza and Arleen listened for a while and then Lorenza started to pull out more from me. Never before did I ever talk about the damage that was done to my sister and me. Never before did I feel so free. Never before did I feel so human.

In all the years that I have been teaching, I have spotted two abuse cases among my students. They were reported and handled. For me, that's two abuse cases too many.

I started having other humanistic experiences right after my second recurrence of breast cancer. I had taken four months off from work. The radiation treatments were making me too tired to be an effective teacher. I hated not being able to work.

Jeffrey and I were driving home from the movies at eleven o'clock at night when I started gasping for air. "I can't breathe, Jeffrey."

"What do you mean you can't breathe, you're talking, you're breathing!"

"Don't argue with me, I'm telling you I can't breathe, get me to the hospital!" We were already driving up our driveway.

"Look, I have to go to the bathroom, then we'll talk." We went into the house. Sometimes being married to a cardiologist has it's disadvantages. Jeffrey was being very scientific with me. If I was standing and talking, then I was okay, I was breathing.

Now this is great, I thought, just like the shoemaker's daughter who goes without shoes, I'm going to die and I am a cardiologist's wife!

"If you don't get me to the hospital," I said, gasping for air, "I'll call the ambulance myself!" I yelled through the closed bathroom door. Flush. Jeffrey opened the door.

"Come on, let's go." His swift movements made me wonder what changed his mind. He went from 0 to 80 miles per hour on the highway.

"I could get you there faster than an ambulance."

"Dead or alive," I muttered under my breath, gasping and holding on.

"This is Dr. Rothburd, get a wheel chair ready for me," Jeffrey called ahead to the emergency room. "I'm bringing my wife in, she's having trouble breathing."

I heard the intensity in Jeffrey's voice. I started to gasp for more air. Another telephone call was made. "Bernie, Allyson is having trouble breathing, meet me at Good Sam."

Jeffrey stopped in front of the emergency room, ran out of the car and into the hospital leaving me sitting there. I didn't know what he was up to. I opened the car door, stepped out and started walking toward the emergency room. Suddenly Jeffrey came running out with the wheel chair, I kept walking. He whirled the chair around to walk in my direction. I was already inside the emergency room.

The nurse got me up on the stretcher. Bernie and his wife, Meryl, with whom we had been out with earlier, arrived at the hospital. Bernie Nash is our very good friend and internist. Meryl came to support me. Jeffrey had already started tests on me to check my heart. He was so sure it was nothing; but on second thought, he wondered if I was having a reaction to my medication. My heart was fine; I wanted to kill him, anyway, for not acting fast enough for me.

"Would you believe I had to wait until he went to the bathroom!" I told the nurse, Meryl, and anyone in the hospital who would listen. The nurse kept rubbing my arm as she injected me with Valium. Meryl spoke softly to me. My breathing felt normal again. I had my very first anxiety attack. Jeffrey kissed me and took me home.

The next evening, Jeffrey's cardiology group was part of other cardiology groups who got together to throw a huge party during the holidays in December. It was being held at a restaurant on the water. Jeffrey wanted to wear his black, round collared pullover with his sports jacket. He couldn't find it, so he started going through every drawer in the bedroom.

"Did Adrienne take my pullover to school with her?" he said continuing to slam drawers. "Why would she do that?" "Why? Because she always takes things and doesn't return them."

"She didn't take your pullover; would you please stop slamming the drawers. I'll go to the mall and get you another pullover." Jeffrey stopped only after he was convinced it was no longer in the house. Feeling a little tired from the night before, I went to the mall to search for a pullover just like the one Jeffrey had. After going to three stores, I found something similar and one that would look good with his sports jacket.

I called Jeffrey on the cell phone while standing in the middle of the mall. "Jeff, I found a pullover for you, it's not exactly like. . . "

"I really wish I could find my shirt ," Jeffrey interrupted. With that, I screamed into the phone, in the middle of the mall, "Wrong answer, Jeffrey, you're supposed to say THANK YOU!"

Jeffrey realized I was having a hard time. "Get in the car and come home, Allyson, " he said in a very gentle voice. I did.

I felt I was falling apart; not working and not being able to concentrate. I was having a hard time and had to learn to give in to my limitations.

The party was jammed with families and hospital staff. I ran into the nurse who helped the night before. I started to laugh and shake my head. "I've seen and heard it all," she laughed, "It's okay, I'm glad to see you're feeling better."

I have not had an anxiety attack in a long time; if I do, we'll handle it.

I have learned that in order to be honest with anyone, I must be honest with myself first. When I felt that I didn't have to hide my past, the freedom that I felt came to me in small steps and then, soon after, in one giant leap I was able to get on with my life.

LAUGHTER GOES A LONG WAY

I was sitting at the kitchen table looking out into my yard, Whitney Houston's voice filled the background silence with "I found out what I've been missing. . . "Whitney's song expressed looking for and finding love. What I was missing, aside from a breast, was not feeling sure about which direction I was heading.

I thought back to November, 2000. I walked into Mrs. Lavelle's office with support from Arleen Gomshay. "Is this a school matter? Mrs. Lavelle wanted to know. I didn't respond as I sat down in front of her desk. "It's a personal matter," Arleen responded for me. Mrs. Lavelle got up, closed the door, and then returned to her seat.

"Come on, Allyson, talk!" I remember thinking, "I have cancer," I said, not even sure that I had just spoken as I sat with my face downward. "I have cancer," I repeated, this time looking straight into Mrs. Lavelle's eyes. "Again. Third time," I continued in a syncopated rhythm. It didn't matter that Mrs. Lavelle stared straight back at me or that Arleen fell silent. "I won't let them give me chemo," I started to ramble on. Arleen interjected, "You don't have to think about that yet." Arleen was retiring that year after spending over thirty years in the teaching profession. I didn't want her to retire, just as I didn't want to go through another round of cancer.

"What can I do for you?" Mrs. Lavelle spoke very softly. I wanted to say "Please make it go away," but I knew, this time, it went through the blood stream and into the bone and that no one could make it go away. "Just keep me busy," was my reply.

"Whatever you need, Allyson," Mrs. Lavelle said as she moved towards me and wrapped her arms around me. I could have stayed in Mrs. Lavelle's loving arms all day. I turned and walked out the door.

Within a month, I knew I had to do something about my mental state. I didn't want to feel like my life was completely over so I did what always came naturally to me. Laugh! Enter Joyce Schwartz. Joyce
started teaching with me in the late 1970's. She left for personal reasons and returned to I.S. 109 around the same time I did. We were standing next to Mrs. Lavelle when Joyce quipped, "By the way, Allyson, when you go, can you leave your car to my son in your will? You know, Jordon really needs a car!" I looked at Mrs. Lavelle's face. My principal, "a class act," didn't know whether to laugh or not. I told her it was okay to laugh. I told her that because I knew I would get the last laugh.

When I got home that day, I immediately called my friend, Judy Engelberg, the attorney. I asked her to do me a favor and make up a mock will leaving Joyce my car for her son. Judy responded, "You are so sick!" then burst out laughing as we thought of all the stipulations that went along with my "gift." I then went to Tiffany's in Manhasset and bought a silver bookmark in the shape of a car, since Joyce was an avid reader, and presented Joyce with "the will" and "the car." I wish I had a camera as I watched Joyce read the will and open the tiffany's box. My "tell em like it is" friend was speechless.

Laughter goes a long way. When I went for my second bone scan nine months after the third recurrence because I was feeling a little pain on my right side, I walked in wearing a button on my shirt that said: *I lived, I loved, I laughed, Now what?*

Sometimes when I don't know whether to laugh or cry I do both.

THE STAGE HAS BEEN SET ALL ALONG
(AND SO I FIGURED IT OUT)

It was really my father who gave me strength and my mother who gave me my independence. My father's incomprehensible actions mixed with his genuine times of caring and my mother's denial of my father's actions, taught me to depend on myself. I knew what I liked and disliked. I liked consistency and sincerity. I disliked the feeling of helplessness and of being afraid.

I didn't know it at the time, but the stage was being set for me all along so that by the time Adrienne was born, it was easier for me to face more challenges, not that I needed any more.

"Adrienne, I just gave you three glasses of water and you're still thirsty?" "You wet your bed again?"

"I'm sorry," Adrienne's pediatrician said, "she has diabetes." Adrienne was four and one-half years old.

"Do you know what that means? Do you know what kind of life she's in for? Do you know about the complications?" Jeffrey was, as they say, talking at me.

"No, I know nothing about diabetes, but I'll learn everything." I said tearfully. I didn't know where to start; I just knew I had to figure it out.

Adrienne's diabetes turned into a family affair. We all took responsibility; we learned about the disease together on all different levels. Adrienne tested her own blood sugars; she even showed her kindergarten
class how to do it. When I finished injecting insulin with the

syringe, Adrienne carefully filled the syringe with saline and injected her dolls. When Jeff and I took a weekend getaway, it was my mother and father who took care of her. My father practiced giving injections into an orange. When we were with friends, they all ate on Adrienne's schedule. We were grateful for such caring people.

Four years later, with the diagnosis of breast cancer, I stood my ground. I could handle it. I had the support of my family and friends. Adrienne was even willing to give up her multicolored clown's wig when I lost my hair.

"You could keep my clown's wig if you want to; and don't worry, I'll hold your hand if anyone makes fun of you." Adrienne knew, even at eight years old, that it is easier for someone when support is shown.

It was the news of my last recurrence that was the hardest for me. "You've crossed the line," I kept hearing in my head. My strength wavered and my fear presented itself in a big way.

FEAR: fear of more metastases, fear of not living long enough to see Adrienne settle down and fear of not living more years with the man who I always loved.

"I'm afraid to die," I finally admitted to myself. I needed to do something, so I did.

The invitation read:

Please Come For:
Ally's 50th Birthday
Ally and Jeff's 25th Wedding Anniversary
Adrienne's 21st Birthday
Your Presence is Our Present
Casual Dress

I looked out into the crowd of a hundred and twenty-five people. There among all the people who made me smile were Jeff and Adrienne and my mother from Florida, looking great, and sitting with my cousins, Ellen and Steve, also from Florida. Ellen always liked to keep the family together. I never knew I had so many cousins.

"This is your twelfth cousin removed, " Ellen would gleam. *"Ellen, no one's removed them . . . yet"*

My sister's husband was there with his soon to be wife. I appreciated her coming, but she could never take my sister's place, even if she didn't try to. I looked at my niece and nephew. I saw my other brother in law, and Seymour Gross, and Linda were at the party as well. A touch of Canarsie. Jeffrey's boyhood friend Jon, and my roommate, Sue, from Hartt College and Peter from medical school were also there.

I scanned the room again. There were the doctors who took us under their wing and introduced us to boating when Jeffrey joined his practice.

"I want to buy a sailboat," Jeffrey couldn't control his excitement as though he just won the lottery.
"Then do it, I laughed.
"Hop on mate."
"Are you sure you know how to sail this thing?"

Our thirty-foot Wanderer, an old sailboat, brought us joy and white knuckles for me for ten years. We sold it and started to travel abroad.

There was Michael Ross (Susan Ross' husband), laughing with his wife, Mindy. Mindy became so much a part of Ben's life without ever taking anything away from Susan and she became my dear friend. The Shapiro's were missing, Olivia sits with me during my two hour treatments. The Engelberg's were talking to the Nash's. There were the Chowdhury's.

" So, Ellen, what did Aram like to do when he was younger?" I asked my friend, whose son, Aram Chowdhury, was killed in a car accident after he just started college.

"Well, he liked to act. He played the part of the little Egyptian prince when he was seven years old in <u>Big Bird Goes to the Museum</u>"

"I know that one!" I couldn't believe what Ellen had said. It was the only videotape I saved from Sesame Street when I cleaned out the drawers as Adrienne grew older. I loved that tape!

"I didn't know that was your son!"

In it, the little Egyptian prince had to find the answer to the question, "Where does today meet yesterday?" Only when he gets the answer can he join his parents in the sky and become a star. The last scene shows Aram walking up a flight of stairs into Heaven after Big Bird and Snuffy help him answer the question. He twinkles down at them. I wanted to cry for my friends, the Chowdhury's.

My colleagues from I.S. 109 were all at the party. It was ironic that out of everyone, I had the most years to complete until retirement. How was I going to do that? I didn't want to think about it; this was a party.

Okay, we're taking Arleen and Lorenza out, you tell Harriet and Phyllis G, and Phyllis A. Don't forget Joan, Carol, Anita, Shelly, Joyce and Betty; don't forget the list goes on and on. No matter what, I.S. 109 always knew it was important to hold on to good times.

Then there was Jeffrey's office staff; the calming crew.

Adrienne's friends were there, all grown up; and there was Adele Stein, Adrienne's first grade teacher, and Donna Lipari, her former voice teacher. I glanced at Conrad Malatak, my neighbor who did the illustrations for my very first book, <u>Grandparents Are Special.</u> Kind is just a mild description of Conrad.

It was because of the friendships of all these people that I was now ready to conquer my fear. Taking Arimedex causes me some muscle pain and tiredness. I just say it's because I'm getting older and need a new mattress. When I can't reach a dish in the kitchen, I say I'm short, instead of my right arm never got back to be able to reach the same height as my left. If mind games help me through, then I play them.

I often wondered why this was so hard for me. Everyone dies sometime. I suppose it's different because I am not ready to die, and I don't know what it feels like to be ready. Is anybody ever ready to die? Do they always want to hold on, no matter what? Is it a conscious act or do they just die? I can't answer my own questions and I always felt that unless you are walking in someone else's shoes, do you fully understand how one truly feels. I can't ask a dead person what it feels like, now can I?

This is where I think of religious people. I have heard many say on different subjects that there are no answers. I have to agree with that. Having no definitive answer helps me. Can you understand that? My death isn't imminent. I don't know exactly how I will feel when I get really close to exiting my life, though I feel much closer than ever before. The box checked for prognosis now reads "fair" not excellent, not good, but fair. Well at least I still have one more box to go.

I love life so much that I will just have to trust that death is only a continuation of life. Since Heaven is too far for me to touch, I like to think that for all the people who died and who I cared so much about, that they act as a reminder to me to perpetuate certain acts of kindness. They still make me smile as they closely walk with me.

My maternal grandmother still reminds me to read to all my students and my maternal grandfather reminds me that a husband and wife should always love each other. My paternal grandmother listens every time I hum a new tune and my paternal grandfather likes it when I go for a walk with someone I just met. Then there is my father who really never meant to hurt anyone and hopes that I can remember more of the good times than the bad . . . I'm trying. I report to my sister all the family news and she reminds me that it is only when you can protect yourself that you can begin to protect others. I'm reminded of the gift of friendship I shared with all those who died of cancer and who touched my heart and I'm reminded that it's how we live our life that counts.

So when my time comes, when I'm told nothing can be done for me anymore, I hope too, that I can remind people to laugh, to love, to trust and most importantly, for my daughter not to be afraid.

EPILOGUE

Allyson wrote this memoir after having an abnormal bone scan. It was presumed this was metastatic breast cancer. This may have been erroneous, as she lived another 20 years without any evidence of breast cancer. The specter of recurrent breast cancer however, was never very far from our conscious thoughts. She worked until 2013 when she retired after 25 yrs of teaching. She continued to be plagued by medical issues, including bowel surgery, complicated by a bowel obstruction two years after surgery due to adhesions. For unknown reasons, her large intestine did not function properly requiring her to have an ostomy after spending three weeks in the hospital during which time I thought she might die. This was a further disfiguration on top of her prior mastectomy. Managing her daily activities was also made more difficult because of the ostomy. Nevertheless, she continued to go about her daily business, we continued to travel and rarely did I hear her complain even though life had become more difficult. She suffered from multiple episodes of kidney stones requiring medical intervention and lithotripsy as a consequence of her ostomy.

Allyson was fortunate enough to see Adrienne get married to her wonderful husband Brian, and bless us with two wonderful grandchildren, Molly and Noah. She babysat for Molly when Adrienne was working and spent as much time as she could doting on Molly. In addition to this memoir, she wrote a diary documenting all of the milestones and memorable moments Molly experienced. She loved Noah just as much.

In 2016, shortly after I retired, she complained of back pain, which we thought was from kidney stones. Sadly, it was not. It was lymphoma. Once again we went down the rabbit hole of chemotherapy, with the nausea, vomiting, hair loss, and debilitation that treatment engendered. She required hospitalization on

three occasions, the most serious after passing out in our kitchen, hitting her mouth on the counter, knocking out her four
front teeth. More disfigurement. She could have easily died, as her
platelet count was so low that had she hit her head she might
have suffered a fatal brain hemorrhage. Her teeth were ultimately
reconstructed by Dr. Dino Pappous, a kind, empathic prosthodon-
tic dentist. Through all of this she was not bitter. She could see a
light at the end of the chemotherapy tunnel and now had grandchildren to live for.

After recuperating and being told that she was in remission, we
resumed our lives, traveling and enjoying our young grandchildren. Her strength and stamina however, were not as before. We
caught up with family, visiting Austin, TX for the epic Sternbaum
Thanksgiving celebration. We spent a weekend at Kalahari Water
Park, as Allyson always wanted to have a family vacation with
Adrienne, Brian, Molly and Noah.

October 2019 brought the final insult. A routine mammogram
revealed a lymph node in her left armpit. While we were concerned about breast cancer, this turned out to be a recurrence of
her lymphoma. She remained asymptomatic for several months,
allowing us to spend some time in Miami Beach in March, 2020,
until Covid 19 caused us to cut our vacation short and cheat us
out of truly enjoying the few remaining months of stable health.
Various treatments ensued, beginning in June, 2020 and in December 2020 a PET scan suggested she was in remission. Shortly
thereafter, however, she began to lose weight and the inexorable
decline, and debilitation ensued leading to her death in March.

In January 2021, she had a conversation with me saying she
wanted this to be over. In typical Allyson fashion, she was concerned that her illness was dragging me and Adrienne down. Un-
beknownst to me, she wrote letters to me, Adrienne, Molly and
Noah, as well as her final plea for more time on this earth which
she knew she was unlikely to have. In this final plea, she for the

first time expressed just how angry she was at her impending death. This letter and the other letters she wrote can be found after this epilogue. Allyson always saw the positive side of everything and everyone. She always felt bad for anyone with less than she had. I always kidded her that she saw the world through rose colored glasses. The only specific recollection I have of this was on our honeymoon. We were in Barbados at a hotel called Sandy Lane. A very British, old style resort. Two story buildings, beach (no swimming pool), breakfast served on your veranda with white linen table cloths, napkins and silver coffee/tea service. On the beach were stacks of beach lounges. I went over to move two of them when an elderly (we were 26 and 25) appearing black man came over to move the lounge chairs for us. I immediately recognized that this was how he made his living and was prepared to let him move the chairs. I also liked the idea of being catered to. Allyson, however, took one look at this man, felt sorry for him and said we would move the lounges ourselves. I quickly explained to her that this was how he made his living. She told me to pay him anyway, but we would move the lounge chairs. This was how Allyson approached life and those she perceived as worse off than herself.

Despite being kind and gentle, Allyson could be a force to be reckoned with. Although she was slight of build (5'2", 95 pounds when I met her, never more than 120 pounds her entire life) and soft spoken you did not as Mrs. Lavelle, one of her principal's said, "want to get her Irish up." You did so only at your own peril.

When we moved to Dix Hills in 1987, Allyson requested a meeting with Mr. Opas, the principal at Forest Park Elementary School, and the staff who would interact with Adrienne, to discuss her diabetes special needs. She discussed administering insulin, her dietary needs and schedule and what to do in an emergency.

One of the teachers asked what if they made a mistake. Allyson's reply was, "you will not make any mistakes with Adrienne!"

On vacation to Israel, Allyson was waiting for me outside Mahane Yehuda, the Jerusalem Central market. It was hot! She was standing under the awning of an outdoor kiosk to shield herself from the sun. Suddenly a woman bumped her. She thought nothing of it, until it happened a second time, when Allyson realized the woman wanted her to move away from her kiosk. Allyson turned to the other women working the kiosk and with words and gestures told her that if her friend bumped her again, she would smash her face into the ground.

THAT was my 5'2", 110 lb, soft spoken, sweet Allyson when you got her Irish up!

Her colleagues at I.S. 109 nicknamed her Lola, because what Lola wanted, Lola got. Don't mess with this chick who appeared so unintimidating.

For several years she served as the union rep in her school. I'll never really know why. She was not an activist. Her friend and colleague Joyce Schwartz had been the union rep before her. Joyce moved up to the district rep position and convinced Allyson to take the job as Joyce would then have a trusted, reliable person in the job.

Allyson had to go toe to toe with her principals on several occasions as part of her job as union rep. The last principal she had to deal with was Shango Blake. An imposing man who ran the school as if it were his personal fiefdom. He had the students wearing uniforms, even though there was no requirement or directive to do so in the NYC school system. He assigned teachers at his whim and often intimidated teachers with observations.

Close to the end of her career, after a heated exchange about a union matter, Mr. Blake informed Allyson that she was going to be observed in late May or June, close to the end of the school year; something that usually was not done. I asked Allyson if she was concerned, since she knew that Blake "played dirty." She told me she wasn't as she was confident in her teaching skills. Sure enough, Blake could find nothing wrong with her lesson or lesson plans, and even remarked, something to the effect, "You really can teach!"

Allyson had the last laugh. Blake was ultimately fired for beating a student and misuse of school funds.

Allyson did not really ever desire anything except the health and happiness of her family. She was never concerned with material things, despite being brought up with relatively little.

She was my champion, always encouraging me in whatever I did. She was truly my better half. She was a fierce defender of our daughter, Adrienne and a doting grandmother to Molly and Noah. She was my first and only love. I will miss her dearly.

Jeff

LAST THOUGHTS,

LOVE LETTERS, WRITINGS AND MUSINGS

Anger

Today is Sunday, January 10, 2021. I've been putting this aside, not ready to write, but now I am.

The world was turned upside down around the time of March, 2019. COVID 19 was the virus that killed millions of people round the world. The world was unrecognizable. It brought out the worst in people and the best. For many people in my family, with Donald Trump as President, it was a time we had the sickest, most dangerous leader of our country. We saw what happened when sick people backed him. We saw what was only important to him. We saw his un-American undemocratic way. Enough – it was never enough. People went hungry, people lost jobs, homes. Schools were taught differently. People of color had always been treated differently. It was frightening (Black Lives Matter). Changes had to be made and Donald Trump and his family didn't care. We are counting on Joe Biden and Kamala Harris and his team to bring back some form of normalcy to our country.

I have never considered myself to be an angry person. I'm **ANGRY.**

I'm **ANGRY** because I'm ill and I'm putting my family whom I love so dearly through hell. On and off since I was 37 years old (1988) I've had cancer (breast cancer and lymphoma).

At this moment no doctor knows why I am losing weight rapidly (today 85 lbs. I'm 5'2"). I get weak. I'm **ANGRY.**

My immediate family consists of Jeffrey, we married in May of 1976, Adrienne, our only daughter, Brian, our son-in-law, our grandchildren, Molly, now 7 years old and Noah, now 4. I love all of them *SO MUCH!*

Jeffrey has always been by my side. He is trying so hard not to throw in the towel for me. I feel I'm throwing in the towel, I'm giving up. I don't want to, so I'm **ANGRY**. Adrienne tries to keep up a cheery face for me. She's so hurt. My son-in-law, Brian has been supportive. My grandchildren are so special to me, I could eat them up. Such beautiful children, inside and out.

I'm **ANGRY**, I make bargains – "let me see that my family will get through this, let me see that things are going in the right direction for them." They seem to be, so why should I be **ANGRY?** Because I am, I want to still be a part of them and I'm slipping away too quickly.

My sister, Brenda, died of breast cancer at age 48. My father at age 70 from cancer of the bladder and my mother at age 89 (a month before she was to turn 90) from metastatic kidney cancer.

I remember when my mother didn't want to eat much, and just wanted to sleep before she died. Things that I'm doing now, I'm **ANGRY**.

Jeffrey, my Charlie Brown, (how I love him so) gave me a very good life. I always appreciated what we had, what we did. Good times, hard times. That's life. But WHAT IS THIS? I'm being killed and taking the people I love down with me.

I have wonderful friends too. Thank you (If I name names, I might leave someone out and they don't deserve that).

I've never done this, but I want the biggest favor – **PLEASE, HELP ME. PLEASE – LET ME LIVE.** Not in pain or with no answer to this weight loss. **PLEASE**, let me move on with my family. Laugh, smile. Please help me get over my **ANGER.** Let me be one of the exceptions who make it.

Anger is a harsh feeling. Something in my personal life I've always tried to let go of. Be the optimist.

<u>HELP</u> <u>ME</u> <u>PLEASE</u>!

Thank you,

Allyson Rothburd

Dear Jeff

2020

Dear Jeff,

Wow- this is hard. We've been married since 1976 and we met January 5th, 21/2 years before that. But who is counting? We met at a "mixer" (they don't have those anymore…now you meet "on line") at Downstate. As you would say, Jewish girls looking for Jewish doctors. Not all of that is true – for me- I hated going to the bars, I never did drink. Anyway, in all the years that I've known you, I want to and I hope you can remember all the very good times we spent together. From me being the chop meat queen, 101 ways to make chop meat, to exploring Manhattan, to raising Adrienne who never gave us a day's trouble (until she was in her 20's, but hey, it could have been worse). What a great kid. We were so lucky with her. What a sweetheart!! And think of this, we were able to watch her grow into being a fine young, married adult with two beautiful children, Molly and Noah, our grandchildren. Yes, Jeff, our grandchildren. How fortunate we are! In between there were birthday, and anniversary parties with friends and family. Adrienne's Bas Mitzvah brought out your yellow socks, not to mention our very proud moment of watching Adrienne doing whatever she had to do calmly and with a big smile.

She married Brian and had a beautiful wedding. We traveled to so many places and yes, I was always a pain until we got there. I hated to fly, but I did it!!

All these times, Jeff, we had good health. We even taught Adrienne not to let her diabetes define her. The sky was the limit (she showed us that, literally, when she didn't tell us that when she was in Australia she went skydiving). However, when she showed you the tape of that you had that look on your face of – "WOW! I wish I did that!

And then Jeff, life threw us curve balls. Hard curve balls. I've had four bouts of cancer:

At 37 years old – breast cancer

At 47 years old – recurrence of my breast can cerAt 65 years old – lymphoma, where the cure nearly killed me.

And now at 69 years old – lymphoma – AGAIN!

What can I say Jeff. You stood by me in all these hard times! No one should have to go through hard times on their own. . . I was lucky, I didn't. Aside from being physically and mentally crushed, I was crushed when I looked at you. Though you are capable of taking care of everything, I think about when I have to leave you and that is the killer for me. We should grow very old together!!!

I'm so happy you have hobbies, friends and most importantly, your family – Adrienne, Brian, Molly and Noah. Molly has become your biking buddy and what a buddy she is! Noah loves to do things too. There's a connection coming. They are both so loveable.

Grandparents are Special – let them always remember you with fond memories.

I always loved you Jeff and always will!!

The Best Daughter

December, 2020

Dear Adrienne,

I always told you, you were *the <u>best</u>* daughter I ever had. To which you would reply, "I'm your only daughter." Though that is correct, you were always my best.

You were sweet and kind and always wanted to do the right thing. You did well in school and I was fortunate enough to be able to stay home and do fun things with you until you were about ten years old, when I went back to teaching. I would take you into Manhattan so you could hear the sounds of the trains and ride the elevators. Yu loved going to the library for activities and story time. You played Suzuki violin and took ice skating lessons. There was nothing that you couldn't do.

Then at four years old, you were diagnosed with type I diabetes. Adrienne, I don't know what to say when I think back to this time. I was so lucky to have a kid like you. Everything about diabetes was on a positive not. You learned that the insulin helps you do whatever you want to do. You didn't cry when you took your finger sticks and injections. You learned to work the finger stick machine very quickly and by the time you were eight years old, you gave yourself your own injections. You gave the injections to your dolls (filled with saline), so that they could do what they wanted to also. You were really something else!

In kindergarten you did a show and tell regarding your finger sticks. At Hamilton College became an EMT, something extra while you were a neuroscience major, and eventually as a profession you became a P.A.

Am I bragging? You bet! You could ski with Dad, jump out of planes, sail and feel for others. You always had a heart of gold.

You had a grandma and granddaddy who loved you so much. You never stood on the long lines to FAO Schwarz with Grandma – right to the front of the line and into the store with her! Granddaddy was able to dance at your Bas Mitzvah, just before he died at age 70. Grandma was able to attend your wedding and get to hold her great granddaughter, Molly. Oh, did she love her. She never met Noah, but she would have been so happy to have met him if she could.

I could go on and on about you. After all, you are my only. But I just want to tell you that I think you make a great mother to Molly and Noah. I hope you and Brian and the kids stay well and are happy and grow together. Life is very challenging, as you know. It's how you handle the challenges that count. It's okay to cry, it's okay to fall down. But make sure you get up and be strong. Enjoy all the little things in life. Look around at nature, listen to someone's joke, find the positive in things. Laugh, stay kind, appreciate what you have.

I'm very proud of you, Adrienne. You are my hero! You always knew how to handle your chronic illness so that it never defined you and now I'll learn to handle my chronic lymphoma so that it won't define me either.

I love you, Adrienne. Always did (you know, when you came out with your little cap on), and always will!!

Love,

Mom

Molly

2020

Dear Molly,

You are my very first grandchild. I loved you from the day you were born! I loved every moment I spent with you. There is a journal I wrote that is for you. I started the second book of the journal. I also left a photo album for you.

I never started a journal for Noah, but I left him a letter and some photos (for your Mom and Dad too) I love him *so much also*!

I always wanted to see you and Noah grow up. Whatever part of that I saw I appreciated.

Be healthy and happy Molly.

I LOVE YOU SO MUCH!!

Love,

Grams. (I came up with the name Grams because it's important to know it's the little things in life that are important)

Noah

December 19, 2019

Dear Noah,

When your sister was born, I started to write a journal for her so that one day she could read it and understand how much I loved her. I didn't start a journal for you. I never even started one for my own daughter (your mommy). But that doesn't mean I love you any less. I LOVE YOU SO MUCH. Every time I think of you and how sweet you are, I just want to eat you all up . . . but then I won't see you, so I can't do that.

When I would babysit for you and it was your nap time, you were so easy. I'd read a book or two to you. We'd play a little, we'd giggle. I would line up all your "friends" in your crib the way you liked it. I told you how much I loved you and you would say "I love you too, Grams." You made my heart burst with pride. One day you called me back as I was leaving your room to tell me I forgot to give you a kiss. Oh my, how could I forget. I think I gave you 100 kisses.

You never cried when you were being left by my house. One time, your dad was in a rush and he just about threw you into our house. There you were left, looking at me and Grandpa with your coat on. We all stood silent for a moment and then you said "I'm going to be here for a while." Noah, you made us laugh so, and then I just gave you a big hug!!!

You always want to know how things work. You know all your trucks by name and your favorite show is Blippi. Blippi has huge orange eyeglasses. About a month ago, you too needed to wear glasses. With or without them, you are just <u>too</u> cute!!

You love doing what Molly does and you can't wait to go on the bus with her to school. This summer, you will be going to the same camp as Molly. You will <u>love it</u>!

You are three years old now, the same age Molly was when I first got sick with lymphoma. It's a cancer that has come back again, but this time I'll be able to do many more things than when I first had it. It came back in a different form. It's called low grade B cell non-Hodgkins lymphoma. There is no cure, but hopefully there are enough ways to keep me going so I can still grab you to hug and kiss you. I'm hoping to watch you grow into a fine young man.

The most important thing in life is to have good health. Then you can make choices for everything else. You can choose good friends, you can choose a profession, but you can't choose what happens to you health wise. I didn't choose my lymphoma, but I will choose to not give up. I can't. I have the best grandchildren anyone can ask for.

Always, always remember Noah, that Grams loves you forever and ever! (Molly should remember I love her too!)

Love,
Grams

2020

Dear Noah,

I'm leaving you with life lessons that I hope you and Molly will learn over time.

1. Be kind
2. Keep an open mind. (Look at things in different ways)
3. Aim high. (Don't give up if you really want something)
4. Think in a positive way. (know that in this world things aren't nice or fair and then there are things that are so wonderful!
5. Be true to yourself (know who you are)

I love you,

Grams

August, 2020

Dear Noah,

I have to tell you something funny. YOU ARE FUNNY!!

The other night, over a week ago, you and Molly and your mommy and daddy and Grandpa and me were having dinner outside on our deck. You were so happy and declared that you were going to sleep here. You made up your mind and no one was changing it.

Molly didn't think you would go through with it and told you that if you wanted to stay a while, but then wanted to come home you could. "No," you said, "I'm staying!" When Molly said that you will miss her and Mommy and Daddy, you insisted that you were staying! AND YOU DID!!!

It was such a pleasure to have you spend the night. You had dessert, we played games, watched a little TV (your Mom gave you a bath here before she left). Grandpa read you a book and I can't even say I tucked you in because you like sleeping over the covers. By 8:35 you were fast asleep!

Grandpa made you waffles in the morning while I helped you get dressed. You loved the toothbrush I gave you and took it home.
You told me you wanted to sleep here 100 days! I would love that, but I really think you would be missed at home.

I love you Noah.

Love,

Grams

Brian

December, 2019

Dear Brian,

Every parent hopes that they raise their children to grow up a responsible, caring adults; when they do and have two beautiful children, we think about how fortunate we are.

I love being with Molly and Noah. They make me laugh. I love the excitement on their faces when they have new experiences. Molly is and will always be her own person. It's a wonderful trait. You need to be strong in this world. Yet, she also feels deeply for others. I hope she doesn't change. She'll mature but basically she's strong, bright, funny and loving.

Noah has a curious mind. I love how he turns every toy over because he wants to know how it works. He is also bright, sweet and lovable.

You have to work at having a good family. Most importantly, your family has to know that they can count on you and that you love them. You're there to protect them when you can.

We never know how long we get to live. When I was much younger, I never gave it a thought. However, in my case, because of my health record, I do. What I think about more is that I hope yu and Adrienne live a long, healthy, loving life together. In reality, there are bumps along the way, but hopefully getting through those makes you stronger. I also hope that yur two beautiful children will always be proud of their parents and their parents will always be proud of them.

When I don't fell well, I think of the four of you and I smile.

Thanks for making me smile.

Love,

Allyson (Grams)

ACCOMPLISHMENTS

Besides raising a wonderful daughter and being the best wife anyone could hope for, Allyson was a dedicated teacher. She loved writing and had published Grandparents are Special in 1999, by ProLingua Associates. The book was used in many ESL classes in the New York City Schools.

In 1985, six months after Adrienne was diagnosed with type 1 diabetes, she had an article accepted to ParentGuide magazine, "My Brave Child," published in August, 1985.

She wrote many other pieces that she was content to save for her family.

ACKNOWLEDGEMENTS

Special thanks to Arlene Gomshay and Phyllis Angelson, and of course my most wonderful daughter, Adrienne, who encouraged me to publish this memoir, made suggestions and proof read the manuscript for me.

This has been a work of love in memory of an exceptional person.

Allyson Rothburd 1951-2021
May her memory always be a blessing

Made in the USA
Middletown, DE
16 June 2021